REOPENING BETER SCHOOLS:

Unexpected Ways COVID-19 Can Improve Education

Aki Murata, Ph.D.

Copyright

Global Citizenship Education Press
Chicago, IL. United States of America.
Copyright © Aki Murata, 2020

Published 2020

DISCLAIMER

Cover Design: Faiqa Artwork
Editing: Tomiko Breland
Author's photo courtesy of Alex Baker

Aki Murata, Ph.D.

Dedication

To my two beautiful sons, Miki and Docky,

who have and will always be my reasons why …

Foreword

In a period when most educators are struggling to cope with current realities and simultaneously plan for the unknown in the 2020-21 school year, Dr. Aki Murata's timely book serves as a call to action for educators to seize the opportunity for school transformation. Being socially separated has impacted our collective ability to empathize with the realities of others. Public debate about the opening of schools is ongoing even as this book is being published. Parents are worried about learning loss and child care. Teachers are worried about health orders. School leaders are grappling with how to best support their teachers to create optimal distance learning education. New school finance constraints are also applying pressure. The American Academy of Pediatrics has weighed in on the social importance of schools (American Academy of Pediatrics, 2020). Education laws such as California's AB77 have been passed with record speed to set requirements for distance learning in response to predictable inconsistencies in remote instruction (Johnson, 2020). Part 1 of this book informs the current and future work of school leaders, policy makers, politicians, and parents. Its rich description of teachers' experience during the unplanned distance learning of the 2019-2020 school year provides much needed amplification of the constraints and realities. By reading with an open mind, the composite description and perspectives of over 50 educators will provoke deeper understanding of the issues at play and simultaneously activate possibilities for the future.

In Part 2, Murata presents a hard truth that was unveiled during remote instruction: collective witness of the consequences and manifestations of inequality in schools and in society. While issues of inequity in education have been well documented for many decades, the "grammar of schooling" has largely remained the same (Tyack & Tobin, 1994). Furthermore, societal issues of access and inequality that were less obvious to educators during in person instruction related to areas such as housing, employment, and health care have been revealed. By interweaving connections between educational research, teacher voices and the emerging social movements that have gained momentum during the COVID-19 pandemic, Murata punctuates the growing awakening of educators that acknowledges the undeniably deep and historical legacy of inequity within education as well as the need for radical change and re-imagination of schooling.

The last section of the book provokes reflection, discussion, and action on topics that have promise for improving schooling. Without dictating specific solutions, Murata delineates essential considerations for those who are ready to seize the opportunity. It is easy to imagine how extensive group discussions about humanizing education will be catalyzed among readers. I encourage each of us to allow our imaginations to run wild with ideas that cultivate learning focused on deeper inter-personal connection and anti-racism, no matter the format.

      Writing a book is a labor of love that often takes years to complete. The speed and depth of Murata's work required tremendous personal sacrifice of time and energy during a period of incredible stress. By accelerating the timeline and publication of this book, she inspires each and every one of us to rethink our past expectations in service of the future.

Onward!

Rebecca Cheung
Executive Director, Leadership Programs
Graduate School of Education
University of California, Berkeley
July, 2020

References

American Academy of Pediatrics (2020, July 7) COVID-19 Planning considerations: *Guidance for school re-entry.* https://services.aap.org/en/pages/2019-novel-coronavirus-covid-

19-infections/clinical-guidance/covid-19-planning-considerations-return-to-in-person-education-in-schools/

Johnson, S. (2020, June 25) California schools must provide daily live interaction, access to technology this fall. *EdSource.* https://edsource.org/2020/california-schools-must-provide-daily-live-interaction-access-to-technology-this-fall/634452.

Tyack, D. & Tobin, W. (1994) The "Grammar" of schooling: Why has it been so hard to change? American *Educational Research Journal 31* (3), 453-479.

Table of Contents

Aki Murata, Ph.D.

Introduction

All of us are witnessing an important historical time. As the COVID-19 pandemic hit the United States in March 2020, we were forced into a sudden quarantine without being able to take a moment to understand what that meant. We quickly abandoned what was familiar and adapted to a new way of living—one that is based on social isolation and physical distancing. As states announced the closures of all spaces where large numbers of people gathered, our schools also closed their physical doors, and teachers and students promptly went into remote teaching and learning mode.

COVID-19 has been said to have exasperated existing problems in many areas of our lives, giving us no choice but to address them. For example, a couple who had been avoiding relationship issues had to face them once quarantined together in small space. Businesses that had been operating with some level of inefficiency had to reevaluate what was important. Schools were not an exception, and many existing challenges were amplified when the pandemic hit.

I have worked as an educator all my adult life; I have played different roles, such as a teacher, educational researcher, teacher educator, university professor, teacher professional development facilitator, among others. The intimate knowledge I had about schools readily gave me a sense of how teachers were struggling to shift into remote teaching overnight and how principals and other administrators were being pressed to create new guidelines and structures for teachers and students, while they had little idea what was happening around them.

Educators are flexible people by nature because they must be ready to face new challenges every day under normal circumstances. I always thought of schools as a microcosm of our society: Whatever society experiences shows up in smaller ways in each school building (e.g., economic downfall, race-targeted violence). Teachers are routinely required and expected to handle problems they may never have faced before. However, COVID-19 has presented a different kind of problem—it stripped away all dimensions of schooling that we relied on (e.g., routines, standards), and educators found themselves needing to construct completely new versions and models of schools. One principal compared it to riding a bicycle while building its wheels. Many teachers were confident in solving problems with students in person; we thought there would always be a classroom, schedules, and routines to depend on, but these disappeared overnight. We thought we would always have physical school communities for emotional safety and learning, but many of us felt lost when we lost these, as well. We are collectively experiencing a whole new level of adversity we have not experienced before, ever.

I wanted to understand how schools are handling these changes, and, more than anything, I wanted to make sure my fellow educators (many are my former students) were doing okay. I posted a request on social media asking to speak to them via a short zoom interview, and I was overwhelmed by the volume of immediate response and interest. I ended up interviewing more than 50 educators (teachers, principals, school psychologists, parents, district personnel, teacher educators, and university professors) in early May 2020.[1] Having spent approximately 6 weeks with remote learning at that point, they were ready to share stories of how school closings had affected them, initial challenges, mistakes made, lessons learned, persisting problems, and what they anticipated for school reopenings. Many educators also

---

[1] Please find the participant information in the appendix of this book.

expressed gratitude to have the space to talk about their experiences with me, as they all felt they had been working nonstop since mid-March, never having the time or space to digest what they had been doing. Some participants called our interviews "teacher therapy sessions"! The interviews created a space for educators to pause for a moment, put words and labels to their experiences, honestly express uncertainties and frustrations, recognize how much they had done, and get validated for their hard work.

Many started the interview by saying, "It has been difficult, but I am lucky because…" to describe the silver lining (e.g., "we have supportive parents," "most students were ready to learn virtually," or "our district had an infrastructure ready to shift to remote teaching"). This is why I love educators, and I feel proud to call them my friends—they are truly courageous people who stand tall when things are uncertain, providing safety for students even when those students bring unanswerable questions.

As I collected their stories, I started seeing threads and themes through their uniquely different yet similar experiences. These are the foundation of this book. I realize we stand in an unprecedented moment, which means the ideas expressed in this book will stay situated in the time frame of "6 weeks into school closing." We have gained so much knowledge during this time, and I have no doubt we will continue to learn how to effectively run schools after COVID-19, but in this moment— when many of us are grappling for the first time with remote teaching and what it means for us and our students — educators' experiences are especially important, and they will become valuable in the future in our new schools.

One advance warning to the readers – I am purposefully writing this as a non-academic book. If you are interested in reading my research work, I trust you can easily find them elsewhere. I have been trained as an educational researcher (by great mentors) and published literature broadly over many years. But this book is not about that. I wanted to bring together the voices of educators and ideas that are important to me in this volume. Being non-academic book does not make it any less important – it's just a different (more direct) way to communicate ideas with the readers. At places, you may find it challenging to read, and if so, I want you to pause and reflect on why some of the ideas disturb you. I have strong opinions, especially when it comes to how schools treat students of color in the United States and how we need to dismantle systemic racism. I value different ideas and welcome any feedback, but I also wanted to be upfront about the nature of this book. I will also provide a list of additional readings at the end in case you want to learn more.

How This Book Is Organized

Part 1 describes the experiences of one teacher, Mia, for the first 6 weeks of remote teaching. Mia is not a real person, but she represents an amalgamation of the educators interviewed for this book. Mia's experiences are interweaved with stories from the participant interviews, so we get multiple perspectives on the events occurring, and we will all have important connections with her as we move forward to discuss school reopening issues.

Part 2 focuses on a discussion of how social disparity among students was widened through remote teaching and learning. The reasons for such a widening disparity are grounded in broader social issues and are connected to the Black Lives Matter movement, which blossomed, not unpredictably, during this historical period.

In the final part, Part 3, we discuss school reopenings, including how to bring together some aspects of our "old normal" with what we have learned during remote teaching and learning, our "new normal," to create better schools.

Aki Murata, Ph.D.

The COVID-19 pandemic gave us unique opportunities to reflect on and rethink our schools. I sincerely hope that we use what we have learned to reopen our schools for a safer, more equitable, and closely connected global community.

Part 1: Mia

Aki Murata, Ph.D.

CHAPTER 1. Mia, the Teacher

Mia is a 39-year-old African American teacher who has taught elementary school for the past 8 years. She is also a single mother of two sons, who are aged 13 and 10. She comes from a long line of educators: Many of her close and extended family members have been educators, including her mom (a school counselor) and her dad (a school principal), who both retired a few years ago. Her brother, Brandon, is also a high school math teacher, and she is very close to him. Though her divorce, 5 years ago, was not easy, she and her sons are rooted in the local community with extended family and friends, and she felt fortunate to have support when she needed it.

After finishing her undergraduate degree in business, Mia worked at a marketing firm for a few years. While her work responsibility increased steadily, she did not feel fulfilled. She became tired of corporate politics in which White male colleagues climbed the career ladder much more quickly than others. Seeing how her colleagues of color complained but stayed on despite unpromising professional futures, Mia was not motivated to continue with the career. She wanted to do something different, something with a sense of purpose. Coming from a family of educators, she had grown up watching how her parents were always motivated despite professional challenges. Mia was not looking for "easy" — she was looking for meaningful. She went back to graduate school and received a master's degree in education, and she started teaching.

Mia's Students

Mia loved the work from Day 1. Being a teacher gave her a sense that she was doing something important, making a difference for the future. Organizational politics still existed, but when she was in her classroom, she felt fulfilled. She genuinely enjoyed seeing how her students learned, and she felt competent when she could guide each student along their learning trajectory. The students' parents were supportive, and she felt connected to the community in general. After teaching second grade for 5 years, she switched to fifth grade, and this is her third year with the grade. She likes working with her 11-year-olds, who are very smart and can carry on high-level intellectual conversations with her about math problems, the novels they are reading, and social issues that are important to them, but at the same time can be totally silly and playful. She loves their youth culture and how they express themselves in the classroom, and she enjoys her time with them.

Oakwood Elementary School is in a large city, and many of Mia's students are persons of color, come from single-parent households, receive free lunches, and/or are English language learners. These things don't bother her — they actually motivate her to care more, because she feels she can have a large impact on her students' lives. The students and their families rely on her for help. She often feels the importance of her job when she makes an extra effort to understand their needs, provide resources (whether they be academic, social, or emotional), and see them being met. She also knows the students and families appreciate her because Mia is a person of color, that they trusted her to do the right things for them. She likes these invisible bonds and sense of community, which give her work a sense of purpose.

Mia's School

Mia's school building is old, with broken furniture, chipped paint, and nonfunctioning windows in every room. Despite multiple requests, Mia never has enough classroom supplies for her students, and she has to buy them out of her personal funds. The bathrooms are not equipped with soap and paper towels, and Mia also has to buy bottles of hand sanitizer for her classroom.

The school has a strict behavioral policy and has a disciplinary team ready to work with students who are considered disruptive. It is the school's way of helping teachers so that they can focus on teaching. The disciplinary team, which includes a police officer, routinely gives strict punishments to students as consequences of disruptive behaviors, and Mia feels these consequences are extreme. Though she has seen other teachers sending their students to be disciplined every day, and not all her students are angels, Mia prefers to attend to problems through building good relationships with the students in her classroom.

Mia's Colleagues

According to the National Center of Education Statistics data collected during the academic year 2017 - 2018, 79 percent of all U.S. public school teachers were White, 9 percent were Hispanic, and 7 percent were Black. For principals, the picture is similar: 80 percent of all U.S. school principals were White, 9 percent Black, and 8 percent Hispanic. Oakwood school is no exception reflecting the statistics, while 90% of the students are persons of color. In her fifth-grade team, she is the only Black teacher, along with three White teachers, and she can easily identify where teachers of color are in each grade level. Her principal, Russel, is White, and the assistant principal, Laurie, is Black. While teachers of color acknowledge each other in staff meetings, summer PD workshop, etc., Mia has not developed close friendship with any of them, mainly because she is always busy while at work, attending to various responsibilities. She wishes she had more time to get to know them, as she knew how that would make a difference in her work life.

Though Mia is happy in the classroom, there is much to be desired outside of it at her school. Mia dislikes the staff room, where other teachers complain often about their students, blaming them for why they are not learning much. She knows how venting has bonded these teachers together, but Mia does not want to be a part of it. Many of her colleagues are White and commute from nearby suburbs. They have little in common with the students, and instead of trying to understand where the students come from, these teachers seem to believe they need to fix the students to be more like themselves (the teachers) in order for the students to be successful, too. Mia recalls having teachers like that in her own schooling and swears never to be like that for her students.

Reflecting on Learners and Classroom Community

Teaching students of color in schools that are products of White values takes hard and conscious work. Being a Black teacher does not automatically make it work for Mia, either, and she knows plenty of Black teachers who teach to fix their students. Mia has also known White colleagues who are vocal about their minority students' learning and go above and beyond to bring the community knowledge in supporting their learning. Because almost every aspect of her school reflects the majority White values (this is not a special characteristic of Oakwood elementary school but of all U.S. schools: please see discussion in Part 2), she knows that when teaching non-White students, she must reflect on her practices every day, constantly reevaluating her approaches so that the students' ideas are expressed and heard without being filtered through the dominant values. She must model, pause, listen, and be genuinely excited when different ideas are shared, so all students can learn how to do it, too. (See Chapter 16 for further discussion of this issue.)

Mia knows that teachers must purposefully help students make connections between where they are and what teachers want them to learn. This happens intellectually as well as socially and emotionally. It has been said many times that if students feel they are not valued for who they are, they won't learn from the teacher. It took Mia a few years in classrooms to really get a grip on this idea, but these days, she uses the first weeks of the school year solely to build the trust in her classroom by showcasing the students and their families. She learned that when there is a community, students are more likely to want to come to school and learn. They care about each other, their well-being, and their learning, and the classroom functions better. If students feel safe enough to share what they don't understand, she can guide the learning of the whole class through empathy. Her classroom feels magical at times, and Mia is grateful to have such a trusting community for herself, too, especially when things get hard in her life. She seeks refuge in her classroom, just as her students do.

CHAPTER 2. COVID-19

Having taught her group of students since September 2019, Mia was feeling good about the community they had created together over the previous 6 months. The fifth-grade content she taught felt familiar now, everyday teaching was fun to her, and she looked forward to seeing her students every day.

In early March, there seemed to be more news every day about COVID-19. The school held a short assembly where the district personnel talked about the virus and what educators could do to protect themselves. Mia's class had their own meeting to discuss what this meant in the school community, and she again felt good about her students taking the information in without being overly concerned. On Friday, March 13, students and teachers were anticipating the spring break coming up the following week.

By midday, Mia received a memo from the principal saying that the state was going into "shelter in place," and that the school was considering extending the spring break for an extra week and instead returning at the end of March. Mia felt

it was an overreaction to the virus, but she handed out the printed communication for their parents and communicated to students that the most important thing was their safety. The students were delighted to have this unanticipated extended spring break, and left the school excitedly.

When Mia got home, her two sons brought her similar news from their schools: They would be off for the rest of the month. For that night, Mia and the boys cancelled their visit to her parents' home for dinner, realizing that her parents were in the most vulnerable group to be affected by COVID-19. As they talked via FaceTime, her father, a retired principal, expressed concern about how his old school might be experiencing many challenges. He planned to get in touch with the staff on Monday to see how he could help. Her mother, a retired school counselor, was more concerned about Mia and her boys, and asked questions about their feelings.

All in all, they all expected this would pass quickly, and they agreed that they should enjoy the unexpected time off from work and school. They talked about going on a picnic together in 2 weeks, at their favorite neighborhood park, once things went back to normal

CHAPTER 3. Constant Expectation Changes

n the following week, Mia is glued to social media as the situation escalates quickly. By mid-week, she receives an email from her principal, Russell, that the shelter in place order will be extended until April 7, and all teachers are expected to prepare materials for students to work from home. Teachers are not to teach new content, but they should provide materials reviewing what students have learned so far. Mia quickly puts together PDFs of worksheets and sends them to the school secretary, to be sent to students' homes. Her colleague, Sue, who also teaches fifth grade, contacts Mia. Sue solely relies on physical books and textbooks and does not have any materials with her at home. Mia forwards the electronic pages of the textbooks for her to use and offers her assistance going forward.

On Monday, March 23, Mia sends emails to the parents of all her students, explaining what to anticipate for the next 2 weeks. She outlines how each family will be receiving a package in the mail with worksheets for the children. Mia will be available via phone and email if the students and families have any questions about what to do. Some parents respond, thanking Mia for the information. Others send a long email with many questions. As instructed by the school, Mia forwards all questions to the school administrative team, while reassuring parents that things will go back to normal in 2 weeks. She also knows some parents don't have computers or use email, and she notifies the school that they need to mail letters to all parents, just in case.

By the middle of the week, Mia receives another email, announcing the school will go fully into remote teaching and learning. Several emails explain how to create a login for Google Classroom and how to upload instructional materials. Mia feels okay about using technology and remembers online courses she had taken in grad school, but she has never taught remotely before. Multiple emails fill her inbox, and she feels overwhelmed by the sheer amount of new information coming at her.

Story of a Principal: Robert

Robert has worked as a principal of an elementary school in Chicago for the past 10 years. He loves his work and values his connections with the school community. He is proud of his staff and knows he has many talented teachers in the building. As the school closure became imminent in March 2019, his focus was on his students' and teachers' safety. As everyone quickly wrapped up the school week and left for the anticipated 2-week break, he was certain he could maintain the same level of leadership during the break and communicate new school safety guidelines in April.

Because he'd built many close, personal relationships in the school community, answering questions was something he had always felt good about, but COVID-19 brought many uncertainties, and he did not feel confident about communicating positive messages and assurance. As the district policies changed every few days, he composed emails to let the teachers know what they could expect. When faced with a lack of computers and internet for some students, he made several personal phone calls to find currently unused devices and had them delivered to the families in need. He also helped set up Google Classroom for each teacher, and when some teachers faced tech-related challenges, he sent IT support to them immediately.

There have been an endless number of questions from parents, and while he is sympathetic, he has also become protective of his teachers, as he knows they need unconditional support from him during the transition to online teaching. In Zoom faculty meetings, he can see the weariness in the teachers' faces as they share their confusion and anxiety, explaining how, with remote teaching, they are no longer feeling competent.

Robert is surprised to see the vulnerability in his most experienced teachers, and he does his best to assure them that their students are learning as much as they can, given the circumstances. Robert is uncertain what the school will look like in the fall, as he has been busy making sense of the things constantly changing in front of his eyes, too. He has strong trust in his staff and knows they will come through — he's just not sure what that means at this point.

Though the district IT department is supposed to be available to help, when Mia calls to ask a quick question, she is put on hold for 45 minutes. Her colleague, Sue, seems to be at a complete loss, as she does not use technology regularly. She calls Mia several times, and Mia does her best to help her, but Sue's problem seems to be beyond technical issues: She is fearful of using technology. Mia wonders how many other teachers are in Sue's shoes, feeling lost about how to start teaching remotely.

The district's expectation is that schools go 100% virtual by Monday, April 6, giving teachers just over a week to prepare. Mia manages to upload some materials on her Google Classroom site, but they seem inadequate, and she feels very insecure. Helping students and parents log on to Google Classroom is another challenge. She's grateful that her students are old enough to know how to use computers (many better than their parents) and manage to do it on their own. Knowing the local community the school serves, Mia knows some families do not own computers or have internet access. She was copied on the parent emails from the district, announcing that the district will provide devices for students if needed.

The district also implemented a new meal distribution plan in which parents can obtain school lunches (and other meals) at pick-up locations in neighborhoods. At the district's request, Mia volunteers to deliver meals and devices to families for the first 2 weeks of the school closure. It feels surreal to meet her students that way, 6 feet away from their front doors, when it was merely a few weeks ago that hugging them was a part of their daily routine.

The governor announces the cancellation of standardized testing for the school year. Mia is truly shocked by this, because she knows the importance of the testing for student learning. In her preservice education and beyond, Mia was told how standardized testing scores were used to evaluate teacher effectiveness – in many instances, she knew some schools were closed due to the low test scores, or some teachers were fired because of them. Mia did not agree with this approach of punishing teachers for the test scores, as she knew very well these scores were a mere reflection of student performance via a particular summative measure, and her students were learning so much more than that. Because of such emphasis, though, she knew how her colleagues taught for the test, and how fearful they were of the test. With that much professional emphasis they had previously placed on the test, Mia has a hard time they could cancel it so readily. To Mia, too many things have changed so quickly — that the pandemic has reframed what people value in education.

Mia feels her responsibility as a teacher has expanded far beyond what she was trained for. She played multiple roles in the classroom before, yes, but now she is playing many more. When she calls parents, it sometimes becomes a therapy session, where Mia provides a sympathetic ear, and she feels sad for how much hardship some families are experiencing. Some parents have lost jobs, some have lost family members and friends to COVID-19, and many are struggling to adjust to the new way of living. There are a few students in Mia's classroom she could not get in touch with for a few weeks. She called the parents, but they never called back. Mia drove by their houses, knocked on their doors, and left notes to let them know she was thinking about them. She is left with a great sadness, imagining what might be going on in these students' lives. Everyone is suffering, but some are affected much more bitterly.

CHAPTER 4. Mia's Remote Teaching

As April progresses, Mia establishes a remote teaching and learning routine for her students. She holds a Zoom meeting every morning, greeting students and explaining her expectation for the day. She tries to make that meeting engaging and interesting by using different themes — one morning, everyone shows up in pajamas, and for another, they wear hats, etc. Mia also keeps the classroom pet guinea pig, Coco, and she has Coco give a virtual announcement and updates on what her life is like during the shelter in place order. They also play games, such as "I spy," where students share what they can find in their environments according to given clues (e.g., something round and blue).

For the first 2 weeks of remote teaching and learning, Mia creates many PowerPoint lessons, accompanied by PDF guidelines for parents, which keeps her much busier than usual. Also helping her own sons with their remote learning, she realizes that that level of work isn't sustainable. So, she gradually relaxes her expectations and starts uploading only basic worksheets and videos for students to follow.

Mia holds small-group meetings every afternoon where her students can talk openly about what is going on in their lives, and she also makes sure that they know she is always a click away to talk. The major problem is, as anticipated, that not all students attend remote classrooms. About 1/4 of the class never logs on, for one reason or another.

Mia's school organized a "wellness" committees, and Mia has been assigned to make regular phone calls to a group of families. Some parents clearly appreciate and enjoy the communication, but others don't have time to talk or never return the call when Mia leaves a voicemail. It becomes more and more difficult to know how things are going for some of her students. She can only hope that they are safe somewhere, have something to eat each day, and can sleep somewhat peacefully. It is a helpless feeling.

Teaching content is one thing, but being an elementary school teacher, she knows the importance of attending to her students' social and emotional needs. At this point, she is feeling that each student is keeping up with the academic materials she posts for them, but they are not learning from each other anymore. She also feels out of sorts because she can't tell if her students are really doing okay emotionally. The intimate closeness with her students she so cherished is gone in their new virtual space, and she doesn't know how to create it again without shared physical space.

A Parent's Story: Vic

Vic's daughter, Val, is in fifth grade this year. Val has always been bright, well adjusted, and social. She has a large and close friendship circle, and she thrives in the presence of others. When school closed in March, at first Val was happy to have a break, even though she missed her friends immensely. She seems to be constantly on her computer, messaging her friends.

Vic's work closed down in March, and while his employer continued to pay him partially for the first 3 weeks, he had to file for unemployment in April. Job seeking is not easy right now, and while his wife, Bea, continues to work as a pediatric nurse, he has been staying home with Val for the past 6 weeks. Life is stressful. Originally from Mexico, he worries about his parents and siblings in Mexico City. He feels fortunate that he can see and speak to them daily via Skype, and things are going okay so far—as long as he doesn't have to worry about his income.

Val appears to be studying online, and Vic does like her teacher, who seems to be caring and professional. She called a couple of times since the school closure, asking how things were going at home. He has little to say — the family is doing the best it can, but things are not perfect. When he calls the school once during the quarantine with a question, the school secretary is short and clearly frustrated at having to take the call. He doesn't like that — he realizes that everyone is busy, but his daughter's education is important to him. Val has asked several times if she could visit her friends, and Vic has said, "absolutely not."

It's interesting how casually other parents seem to be taking the situation. Maybe because he came from another country, he is very aware of how his actions can affect others in a global sense. He thinks Americans are selfish in general, only concerned about their own immediate needs and happiness. He worries Val is exposed to these American values, and he wonders at times if they should go back to Mexico City to be closer to his folks, though he knows very well Bea would not even entertain the idea. He also hears the news that Latinos are affected by COVID-19 much more than White peers in the United States. He is grateful that he still has a health insurance through Bea's work, but knows he may not receive the best health care in his neighborhood, given that he lives in a poor part of the city. Being socially isolated, he feels tormented by the social inequity he has to live with every day, and dreams about going home, missing his families.

CHAPTER 5. Other Lives around Mia during "Shelter in Place"

For Mia's own sons, Derek (13) and Will (10), she is seeing different approaches to remote learning, too.

Derek: Mia's Older Son

Derek's middle school teachers seem to be coordinating their work well, and he has plenty to do every day, though the level of academic content is low in general. They appear to believe that more structure will help create new routine, thus safety, and provide Derek very detailed schedules and timelines to finish his work every week. For example, he has four to five Zoom lessons every day, where his teachers appear to take attendance.

Mia also realizes that Derek's teachers transitioned into very traditional top-down pedagogy, and he is merely following the instructions given online. Anticipating high school in September, Mia knows this is an important period of her son's life, yet she does not see much new learning happening, and

Derek is often bored and waits until the last minute to finish everything.

Will: Mia's Younger Son

Will's fourth grade teacher disappeared as soon as they shifted to remote teaching. They did not receive any guidelines from her, and Will had nothing to do school-wise for the first week of remote learning. On Monday, April 13, they received an email from the school principal saying there would be a substitute teacher for Will's class, as his teacher would no longer be teaching that year.

The substitute teacher, Ms. Ellen, seems to be a novice. She posts many fun worksheets and holds Zoom sessions where she reads books, sings songs, and draws pictures. To Mia, it feels as if Ms. Ellen is babysitting the class rather than teaching it, but she decides to be supportive of her; Mia sends an email to thank her for the hard work and offer to help if needed, because she knows everyone is doing the best they can right now.

Will is bored, though, and finds ways to play video games on the side while Zoom lessons are in session. Mia catches him doing it and has a talk about the seriousness of remote learning, but she also knows students would do what they find meaningful, and learning remotely might not be on top of their lists right now.

Teacher Maxine's Story

This is Maxine's fifth year teaching seventh grade math. After completing a bachelor's degree in engineering, she joined Teach for America and started teaching at an inner-city school in NYC. Teaching turned out to be much more challenging than she first anticipated, and she often felt like an imposer among her peers, many had completed teaching degrees at state colleges. She promised her partner, Bec, that she would only teach for a few years before getting a "real" job in the engineering field. Maxine did not mind teaching, but always felt her real job is somewhere else.

They adopted twin boys last year, Josh and Aaron, who just turned three in January. Both Maxine and Bec fell in love with the boys right away, and they became a very busy and happy family of four. Bec's job sometimes requires her to travel, and in these times, Maxine finds herself at home caring for the boys alone. She feels appreciative how her community school has a day-care center in the same building, which allows Maxine to drop them off and pick them up at her convenience, with a reduced fee. She is friends with all caregivers at the center, and feels connected to the community.

When COVID-19 hit, Maxine was just as confused and surprised as other teachers. Using district guidelines, she uploaded her teaching materials online and spent many hours figuring out how to use new virtual remote teaching tools. As a middle-school math teacher, Maxine has a large number of students to teach (154 in total). In collaboration with other math teachers in the department, they created common lessons and video-based activities for the students – in a way, Maxine felt it was the first time they collaborated meaningfully as a team, and she enjoyed getting to know the team.

Bec started to work from home right away, too, and the company required so much from her that she had to stay on the computer all day. They live in a small apartment, and Bec set up her office as a part of their bedroom so that she could close the door during the work hours without disruptions. This made Maxine fully responsible for the boys (and her work), when the boys need constant attention.

Maxine is responsible for Zoom lessons on Tuesday and Thursday mornings, but learned that things might not always go as planned. Since all learning materials are uploaded on Google Classroom already, in the Zoom lessons, she briefly connects with students and provides guidelines for what to do. While she never used a TV as a babysitter, she resorted to turn it on during the lessons so that the twin would be engaged with it and not disturb her. But things are never perfect. The boys seem to sense when Maxine is busy and demand her attention. She had to cut these lessons short a few times, and even pre-recorded the lessons the night before for asynchronous viewing when the boys became sick.

It is almost impossible to teach and parent small children at the same time. She is fearful that her students' parents may complain how Maxine is not logging on for the scheduled lessons on time, or not keeping up with the students' work. She is not sure how her colleagues are doing, but she is also the only one with small children in the team. She wishes Bec would be more helpful with the boys, often feeling lost having to do so many things all by herself.

Brandon: Mia's Brother

Mia's brother, Brandon, teachers at a private school in the suburb, and his story is different from hers. Because the school provided an iPad for each student in the fall, when they shifted to remote learning, they already had a familiar structure in place. Brandon already had a website, where he was posting assignments, updating students, and sending messages, so shifting to remote teaching for him simply meant moving everything to his site and providing additional support for students. His remote classroom went on LIVE as soon as the shelter in place order was in effect, and Brandon mentioned to Mia that things were going very smoothly.

The school scheduled each subject area one day of the week, and being a math teacher, Brandon's responsibility is to post a video on Thursday mornings for his geometry students, explaining the tasks for the week ahead. All the work is then due the following Thursday, and he responds to email inquiries during the week as they come in. He organizes small-group Q&A sessions where he could provide targeted instruction for some students he feels would benefit from it. In a way, he feels remote teaching works well for his high school students, as it gives them flexibility and independence; they get to choose when to work and how much work to accomplish. It prepares them for college, where many courses are taught online.

Brandon feels his workload increased somewhat, but his work time is spent in front of a computer instead of in the classroom, and he could work when he wants to. He enjoys the relaxed pace of remote teaching and feels he could go on forever with it.

Mia feels a little envious when Brandon talks about his teaching situation and says so in their phone conversation. She feels strange as her brother describes how he is enjoying remote teaching, as she often feels miserable with it, missing the connection with her students so much. She says he got it easy because his students are coming from affluent families and they have stronger family support than Mia's students. He becomes defensive, saying she doesn't understand how much work he is putting into setting up the lesson materials, communicating with students and their parents, and making sure his students were engaged. After having been a high school teacher for two decades, he thinks he deserves to be sitting in front of a computer for a while, where he can use his content knowledge to create learning materials. Mia knows there is no value in arguing with him, as his school is very different from hers.

Aki Murata, Ph.D.

CHAPTER 6. Anticipating School Reopening

Earlier in the shelter-in-place order, Mia was still somewhat hopeful that she and her students would go back to the classroom before the end of the school year — until the district announced in mid-April that school would be closed for the remainder of the academic year. Though she'd been afraid of the possibility for a while now, she feels a great sadness in realizing that she will never see her current students again in the classroom. Spring is always a time of celebration (after standardized testing, etc.), and she and her students always had several events planned to acknowledge the hard work they put in for the year, celebrate all the accomplishments, and mark the end of the elementary school years. Her students would be moving on to the nearby middle school in the fall, and it will be unlikely that they will spend time together again. Mia feels really sad about that, for her students and for herself.

She is also aware that when the school reopens, in whatever format it will be, she will meet a new group of fifth graders who had been learning remotely for the past 6 months. She knows she will have to put in more effort than usual to establish the classroom community, and she feels weary about facing questions she knows she won't have answers for. But she also knows she will do it — it somehow feels familiar, like when Trump was elected as president, or when school shootings happened: She had to reassure her students that they were safe with her, even though she was not able to completely answer every question with certainty.

Content-wise, the students would be academically behind other fifth grade classes she had worked with before. She knows she will have to start where students are, but she knows little about fourth-grade content, and she feels weary thinking about the extra work learning to teach the new material. Though Mia enjoys teaching, she feels that teachers are tasked with additional work every year, and it makes her anxious thinking about a huge amount of extra work coming her way before the school reopening.

She's also started hearing about additional budget cuts in the district, and how some teachers may be laid off before September. She makes a mental list of people she should talk to, who are relatively sane and reasonable in stressful times, to go over her concerns and worries. She thinks that she should also reach out to her therapist to see if she offers virtual

sessions, because she feels she needs mental health support

in her life more now than ever.

Principal Sara's Story

       Sara took the principalship of the elementary school in the large city in Western United States this academic year, but she is not a stranger to the school. Having worked at the school for many years as a professional development coordinator and coach, she has known all the staff very well and is well respected in the community. She is proud to be a part of the school where many teachers are committed to teaching children in the low-income neighborhood community (with 50% food insecurity, 15% homelessness).

       Instruction-wise, she is hearing teachers and students are doing well in remote teaching and learning. Some teachers shared the student work via Seesaw, etc. with her, and Sara understands how an already-existed instructional norm, grounded in problem solving, helped teachers and students to continue to learn via remote instruction, while the lessons are now spread over a few days/lessons instead of one. Teachers are using Zoom breakout rooms to work with small groups of children, to attend individual students' learning needs.

She feels her job is different now. The principal's and teachers' responsibility became multi-fold overnight for the remote teaching. She feels successful how the school created family support teams, pairing a support personnel (e.g., teachers) with individual families, where regular communication is maintained, guiding the families to resources that they would need (e.g., gift card, food delivery, shelter).

Sara is most concerned about the mental health of the school community right now. They have a pre-K program for children with autism, and she is uncertain how the program can continue through remote teaching and school reopening in the fall. Mental health services need to be in place for students and teachers as the school reopens, and she hopes the teachers keep pushing for academic excellence.

She is aware that she is new to the position, and in district Zoom meetings, she is eager to learn from other principals and what is going on in other schools in the district. She requested additional administrative staff to assist her for the fall, as she anticipates there will be more work to be completed that she does not even know what it is right now.

Aki Murata, Ph.D.

Part 2: Amplified Social Disparity During COVID-19 Pandemic Remote Teaching and Learning

-- Black Lives Matter –

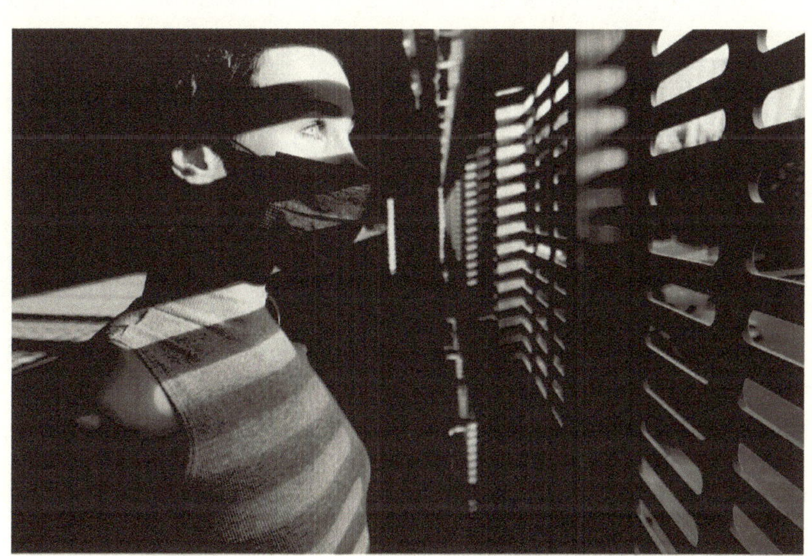

CHAPTER 7. How Social Disparity Widened During Remote Teaching

All educators I interviewed mentioned, in one way or another, how they were concerned about the widening disparity among their students with remote learning. When remote teaching started, for many school districts it became apparent that certain segments of the student population disappeared. These students did not have computers at home or the internet connections necessary for remote learning, and many districts quickly came to a plan to deliver laptops and hotspot devices to communities and families. Many families took advantage of the services, while others remained hidden for different reasons. When life is difficult, reaching out to schools for additional help for their children may not be on the top of families' priority list. As I write this, in June 2020, it was reported that 115,000 students were in need of computers for remote learning in the Chicago Public School system (the largest proportion of these students being

Black and Latinos), and the CPS is still unable to contact more than 2,259 students to determine whether they had any digital access.

Though some students were indeed ready from Day 1 of remote learning, showing up with their own laptop and home internet, other students completely disappeared. As educators, we often come to know each student's home situation well, and that can multiply our concerns. Some teachers seriously worried about the well-being of their students and how they might be facing life-threatening situations away from school. An African American middle school U.S. History teacher in Florida, Mr. Kelley, mentioned receiving an email from a student wishing they can return to school. "Some students have family issues at home and prefer to be in school with their peers and teachers." He said he had become keenly aware what an important role he had been playing in his students lives. The personal connections his students felt with him were crucial.

One San Francisco elementary-school teacher, Molly, mentioned how she felt "unfair" in anticipating school reopening in the fall. As a graduate of a prestigious university, some of her friends send their children to private schools. These children were learning fine through remote learning, if not more. In the fall with school reopening, these affluent schools will be ready to restructure the physical space to accommodate all students, increasing the number of instructional staff to create a *desired* new normal. For her own children and her students, it felt like a very long path until they would get caught up. Because she believes in public education and chose to teach in public schools, she could anticipate multitudes of additional challenges showing up upon reopening. She may be forced to continue to teach remotely a while longer in the fall, while students' social and emotional learning is put on hold. She also mentioned the possibility of home-schooling her children in fear of a higher risk of exposing them to the virus in the public school settings

COVID-19 and the shelter in place order affected all students, but groups with different socioeconomic statuses experienced it differently. For students who had a physically secure home base, with parents who might have switched to work from home and with laptops and internet connections available, the transition was relatively manageable. Though there was undoubtedly some confusion, and it required time for them to become adjusted to learning from their living rooms, many such students got caught up quickly and could follow remote instruction relatively well. They missed seeing friends and being in a familiar school environment, and if we ask them (and their parents), they certainly can discuss many issues with remote learning, but compared to other peers who did not have safe home environment, these students were fortunate. I have interviewed parents who actually said they preferred remote learning for their children, as they could provide one-on-one assistance for them. One parent mentioned she felt remote learning fit her 11th-grade son better, as he could study at 2 am if he wanted to and it gave him new ways to be independent and responsible. For asynchronous virtual lessons, he could pause the video, look back on materials he didn't understand, and come back to the video when he was ready. It allowed him different ways to deepen his understanding of the content. "He is getting ready for college courses this way, anyway," the parent said.

Many schools that served working-class low-SES communities established programs where teachers (and other school and district personnel) regularly get in touch with families (often by phone) to make sure everyone had food, medical attention, financial assistance, and so on, during remote teaching and learning. Overnight, teachers' jobs expanded beyond classrooms as they started to play roles as tech support, social workers, therapists, and more. Teachers shared how, during these phone calls, parents were in distress and had no one else to talk to—the teachers often felt inadequate and in need of additional training.

In other cases, some teachers reached out to families despite their schools and districts discouraging them from doing so, just so that they could make sure each student was safe and protected. Many school districts created food pick-up and delivery services for students, because for some students, school meals were the only food they had every day. In delivering food, one district staff member shared how she had stepped into a small apartment with a grandmother and several school-age children sitting on a queen-size mattress in the middle of the living room, with no other furniture. The challenging living situation existed before COVID-19, indeed, but the quarantine order is making it visible to others. Facing such a reality hurts many of us, and we can no longer ignore the needs of the families. If we don't address the social issues that came to the surface of our lives at this time, the disparity will continue to widen and gets worse in the future.

Aki Murata, Ph.D.

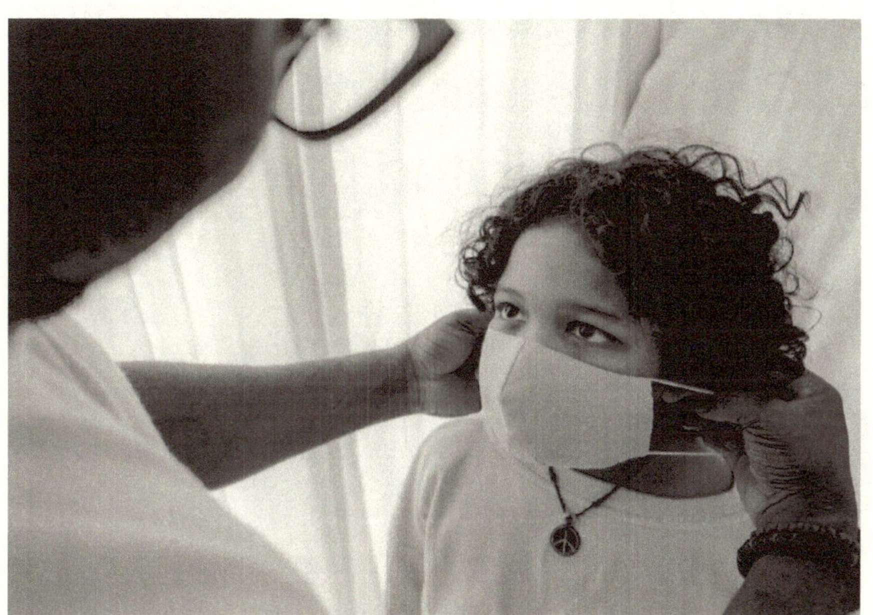

CHAPTER 8. Why Communities of Color Are Highly Vulnerable in the United States

COVID-19 hit people of color much harder than White counterparts in the United States. According to the most-current report by CDC (Center of Disease Control) in July 2020, Black and Latino residents of the United States are three times as likely to become infected as their White neighbors, and twice as likely to die from the virus. The differences are even more stark with ages: Of Latino people who died, more than a quarter were younger than 60, where among White people, only 6 percent were that young. This is not because the virus purposefully targeted persons with darker skin, but because of a long-standing broken social infrastructure. People of color are more likely to live in low-income communities, often in areas where people physically live close to one another. The lives in these communities are tougher, compounded with many sources of stress. The lack of a universal health care system in the United States pushes poor people out of medical facilities, too, while many suffer with chronic illnesses (often over generations) and receive inadequate medical care. Fast food restaurants and liquor stores are often abundant in these neighborhoods, compared to organic grocers and health-conscious restaurants that proliferate in the more affluent parts of a town. Racial profiling is a common practice, and police brutality is often witnessed.

Because of the funding structure of most U.S. schools, which uses property taxes as a primary funding source, low-income communities have poorly funded schools; they are more likely to be equipped with unsafe building materials, outdated technology and resources, and less-qualified teaching staff. The children receive a lower-quality education, without adequate college preparation (and if they do go to college, the lack of support makes it harder for them to continue), and many end up with low-paying jobs. The structures are solidly in place to perpetuate this inequitable system, and children who grow up in the communities usually stay and continue the pattern. It is very hard to break the cycle, as changing one part of the system invites other parts to maintain the pattern. People of color live under much greater stress in the United States.

When the pandemic hit, people of color were among the first to lose jobs because many of their jobs (e.g., retails, factories) could not be performed safely from home. Close living quarters made the transmission of the virus easier. Communities of color lost more lives not because the virus looked for them, but because they were also more likely to have existing health complications that made them more vulnerable. Hospitals are also more likely to turn them away when they show up, providing instead the necessary care for White citizens. The magnitude of the challenges our students of color experienced during the pandemic (e.g., more family members' lives lost, more stress from their parents losing jobs, food insecurity, lack of connections to schools through remote teaching and learning) were primarily results of the existing social system.

Prior to COVID-19, schools in poorer school districts already dealt with many more challenges than their affluent counterparts. While they struggled to hire qualified teachers and maintain safe physical environments, they also faced multitudes of social problems students brought from their immediate communities, such as food insecurity, unemployment, addictions, violence, among others. For many students, schools provide the only safe spaces in their lives, giving them much more than academic instruction but also food and mental health services, and teachers play critical roles as dependable adults who provide daily routines and guidance that the students desperately need. Remote teaching hit these schools harder as teachers' roles expanded into multiple dimensions beyond already full capacities.

CHAPTER 9. The Perpetuation of Inequity in U.S. Schools (in the Land of Equal Opportunity)

Inequality has always existed in classrooms for students of color, well before the COVID-19 pandemic, and even when these classrooms are led by well-intentioned adults. As discussed in the previous chapter, students of color are likely to live in poorer communities, which means they are more likely to attend schools less equipped and with limited funding. Even when the students attend integrated schools where children from different socioeconomic communities attend together, subtle racism can keep students of color from having equitable learning opportunities.

Empirical research findings show how minority students are routinely punished for minor behavioral problems ("acting up") in schools, while White students who behave in the same way are "just being kids." Boys of color are taught early how to behave in certain ways so that they won't be perceived as a threat by White people (e.g., smile, be respectful, no hoodies on head, no hands in pockets). Girls of color are also taught early how to behave in certain ways, so they won't be perceived as overly sexual and suggestive. It is as if these children are being forced to wear "masks" in public so they won't invite unnecessary trouble, but this also sends a message to youth of color that being themselves is not good enough for others — that they need to pretend to be someone else to be accepted (and safe). Many find it completely exhausting to navigate differing standards and expectations in White spaces (schools), just so that they won't be harmed physically and emotionally.

Students of color are also often intellectually invisible in the classroom. Starting in lower elementary grades, well-intentioned teachers often put students of color in lower ability groups, thinking they are doing the students a favor by providing lower-level learning materials with which the students can be successful. And once you are placed in lower-ability groups, you are more likely to stay at that level. Remaining in lower-level groups year after year, students become bored and discouraged from thinking creatively. When students of color speak up in classroom discussions, their ideas are often taken as unimportant, while White students who share the same ideas can be praised and recognized.

Growing up in U.S. schools, many students of color receive subtle messages that it is "okay" for them not to be smart, as long as they can play basketball and other sports well, etc. For students of color to get intellectual attention in schools, it takes more than just being smart and doing their work — it requires conscientious teachers who self-reflect on their own biases and make an extra effort to teach minority students equitably every day. Without such teachers, students of color learn quickly not to speak up when it matters, do the minimum work, and play the "school game." White peers are also racially socialized at the same time, learning how not to treat their friends of color as intellectual beings, as if there is something inherently lacking in them.

When young, students still enjoy the reliable routines, friendship, and connections in the school community, but many students become turned off by the different treatment they repeatedly receive from adults over time. Many students of color end up dropping out of school in middle and high schools.

Considering these inequitable school settings, when the COVID-19 pandemic hit and schools went into remote learning, it is understandable if some of these students were not motivated to keep learning in this unpredictable new learning mode. Virtual classrooms made it easier for  students of color to physically disappear (when they were already intellectually and socially invisible in physical schools), and it caused the disparity, in terms of learning opportunities, to widen further.

CHAPTER 10. Black Lives Matter

Though the Black Lives Matter movement was not a part of the educator interviews that were the main source of data for this book, I want to include a discussion of it as the movement took a leap during the pandemic. I cannot say I was surprised how the movement caught attention (again) all over the world, in particular now during the pandemic, but I am surprised by its intensity. As discussed in previous chapters, COVID-19 hit communities of color much harder than white counterparts'. Topping that with police brutality was just too much for many of us and for the current movement, many white people are vocal in demanding changes. It makes me feel cautiously hopeful to know protesters are everywhere in the world, marching for valuing Black Lives, and that uncomfortable but important conversations are happening among people with different backgrounds — including among White people. Institutionalized racism is a backbone of the U.S. society, and the system was placed there purposefully to keep society privileging White people. Coming from a different culture myself, the amount of hatred I have seen White people have toward black and brown skin is astonishing in the United States. Such racism is learned through lived experiences, and unlearning it will take time, but it is not impossible.

I am a child of mixed heritage, coming from a long line of diverse genes. While I was born and grew up in Japan, all my relatives from both my mother's and father's families looked somewhat different because they had foreign blood mixed in at some points. And I grew up hearing the stories of discriminations from various members of the families. Japan is a primarily homogeneous country, and Japanese people in general hold strong prejudice against others who are different. When everyone in my immediate and distant families belonged to the "different" group, I was constantly aware of my uniqueness while growing up and tried my hardest to be like others. It is no accident that I moved to the United States as an undergrad, and I continue to find myself to be the only "different one" in many situations. I am naturally drawn to marginalized groups and people who are different, and I found, over many occasions, it is disheartening to see how people of color are treated in this so-called land of equal opportunities.

Even before the COVID-19 pandemic, so many lives of color were lost because of unnecessary police brutality, and the weaponization of Whiteness is truly astonishing. (See, for example, the video of Amy Cooper calling the police on a Black bird watcher and lying about assault when he asked her to leash her dog.) I have experienced racism myself in the United States, and I am sad to say I have developed a keen sense of when someone looks at me or talks to me with condescension or racist undertones. I have learned it does not matter how many degrees I have or how much education I have attained; to them, I am someone inferior and unpleasant because of my race.

It is not the first time we as a society are screaming at the top of our lungs, "Black Lives Matter!", but I think that what is different this time is there are more White allies joining the movement. Because White people are the ones who benefit from systemic racism, I have always known that without their taking a primary lead, the movement would not go anywhere. When privilege is invisible to them, there is no reason not to stay comfortably within it. A White friend of mine hesitantly disclosed the reasons she felt compelled to join the movement this time: She had already been feeling vulnerable with COVID-19, and seeing the video of George Floyd brutally murdered by police in Minneapolis, she empathized with Black people's pains in a different way. She also shared how she felt more comfortable now, seeing other White people posting all over social media about the movement.

The Black Lives Matter movement has called for a number of police reforms, including the defunding of the police, utilizing unarmed professionals for nonemergency help, retraining the existing police force to create a new culture, and hiring new police officers. These are all positive changes in the right directions, but systemic racism cannot be dismantled unless all of us take extra effort to reexamine what we do and how our Black brothers and sisters are treated in our society. Education is one of the key places to start this reexamination, to cultivate new awareness among our children and youth so they will be strong agents of change in the future with our continuing effort.

CHAPTER 11. Now Is a Perfect Time to Make Changes

Student diversity has existed in U.S. schools for centuries. The historical landmark Supreme court decision made in 1954 with Brown vs Board of Education ruled it illegal to segregate schools according to students' races. Yet the debate still continues to this day whether or not to educate our children differently according to their racial and cultural backgrounds. We are a country of immigrants, and different families brought different cultures, languages, religions, practices, and ways of living to this land. It is easy to pay lip service to how we value our differences, but in practice, many of us are fearful of others who do not share the same backgrounds and react defensively when faced with ideas different from our own. Though many schools talk about celebrating diversity, it may merely mean one "culture day" celebration in May, or a librarian recommending books about African-American history in February. We all knew we could do better in this area, but we kept ourselves busy with other issues that we preferred to deal with and ignored the problem much too long. COVID-19 brought this important problem upfront, and this is not the time to talk clean. We must get messy together to address the educational inequity in our country.

Diversity, when used positively, benefits our schools in many ways. I have researched internationally how students learn more when different ideas are discussed in classrooms, as they critically evaluate their own thinking process instead of merely following teachers' prescribed methods (See the suggested reading section). We need diversity to move our society forward, and school is the place where our youth are learning how to do that. We must bring a stronger message to our classrooms that students who come from different communities and different backgrounds are welcome, or even necessary, if we want to learn new things every day.

In U.S. schools, we provide different educations to different groups of students, in the name of individualism and community-based needs. As early as in 1980, research studies found schools in different neighborhoods provided education precisely targeted for the populations in the community – e.g., working-class children received rule-based education, while upper-class children received education focused on free investigations (Anyon, 1980, 2014). Our education system continues to serve our children in stratified manners, while we are aware that society will not be able to sustain its productivity when merely half of our workforce is equipped with basic academic skills. The COVID-19 pandemic has taught us much about how we must work and live as a global community in order not only survive, but thrive; it reminds us that we are not living in a vacuum. If we want to remain healthy, we must care about the health of our next door neighbor and the people who live on the other side of the globe. Education is the same way: If we want to continue to grow as a global society, we must educate all our citizens.

The purpose of education is to prepare our children to become members of our society. As the COVID-19 pandemic illustrated, all of us needed to work together to minimize the spread of the virus. If only one community quarantined itself while others were open, the result was a failure. It is the same with education: We must raise the bar across all schools so we will all benefit from the effort, or we will all fail. In U.S. schools, we have always asked stratified questions, like "what are we teaching, and to which students?" COVID-19 vividly reminded us how that approach is wrong. If we truly want to exist as a human race and value our well-being as a society, we will have to start asking a different question: "What do we teach all of our students and why?"

In reimagining schools reopening, educational leaders will want to communicate authentically and transparently what they are planning for their new school. COVID-19 offers an ideal space to do that because none of us knows the answer. As we try new things, make mistakes, and learn, the learning should be openly shared and discussed among key education stakeholders, so others can build on collective learning. If schools in affluent areas are the ones ready to make mistakes first, schools in poorer areas can learn from those mistakes when they begin their own process.

We are tired of talking about how much we value collaboration—COVID-19 really gave us an opportunity to become vulnerable, admit what we don't know, and honestly collaborate as we all figure this out together. Open up conversations. Ask questions that we don't want to ask in fear of looking clueless. We are truly in this together. Let's learn together and create new schools together.

Part 3: Reopening Better Schools

Aki Murata, Ph.D.

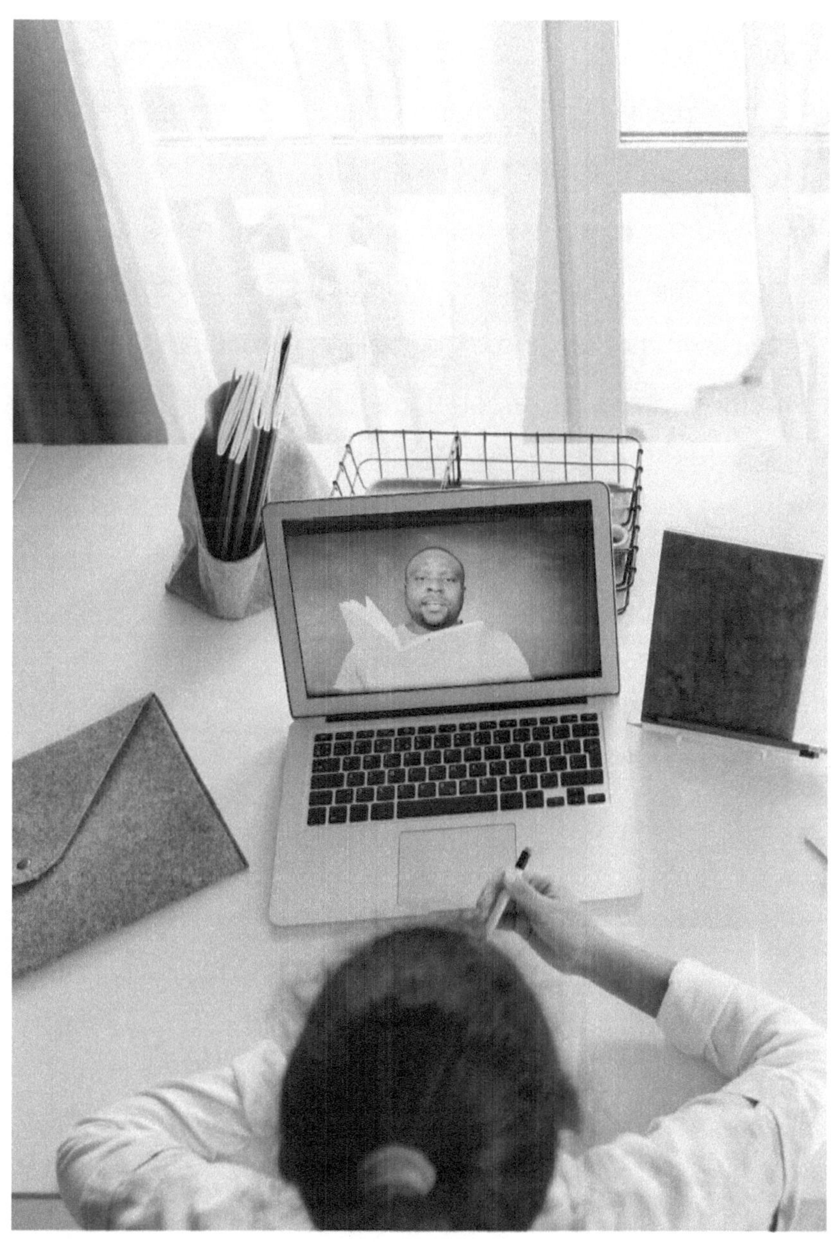

As this book is being published in July 2020, we are having yet another discussion on the timings of school opening in the United States, facing the new surge of COVID cases across the country. CDC is revising its recommendation weekly, and each state is coming out with their own models and expectations. I anticipate new guidelines are provided every week of the summer, and I want to make it clear that the ideas shared in the chapters below will be applicable "when" the schools reopen, be it this fall or next spring.

Aki Murata, Ph.D.

CHAPTER 12. Three Dimensions of New Schools

Reimagining schools reopening after COVID-19 remote teaching, school leaders will need to consider three distinct dimensions:

1) the physical organization of new schools

2) academic content

3) social and emotional care

Though these dimensions will interact and work together, focusing on one and not the others will invite many challenges later on. I discuss the three dimensions separately in this chapter, followed by a more focused discussion of Dimension 3, as I consider social and emotional care (which supports the other two dimensions) to be the most important dimension of the school reopening.

Dimension 1: The Physical Organization of New Schools

When we think about new schools and how they might look upon reopening, it's easy to become overwhelmed. In order to ensure the safety of our students and teachers, we will need new protocols and physical safeguards in place before welcoming them back to the school building. With the COVID-19 virus so easily transmitted between people, physical organization and spacing will become very important, or we will only end up closing schools again. This is where we can learn from other countries who have opened up their schools already. UNESCO reports that schools have been closed in 146 countries worldwide due to COVID-19, affecting at least two-thirds of student globally. One thread in different reports from different countries is that they have seen very little outbreaks among children when schools were reopened purposefully and carefully. Their successes and failures should inform our decision-making, and I will add different scenarios in the following sections.

Three Dimensions of School Reopening

Physical	Academic	Social/Emotional
Health Monitoring Masks, gloves, and hand washing Physical distancing in classrooms Deep cleaning of school facilities	Start where students are Trust that students will get caught up with time Use virtual tools purposefully	Communicate safety messages Take time to establish safe communities Looping with same teachers when possible Individual and group counseling time

		Global citizenship and anti-racism education

1). Health Monitoring

Temperature checks at home and at schools will become vital. Body temperatures of every person who steps foot on campus (students, teachers, and other staff) should be taken every morning at home, and again upon arrival at schools. When running a temperature above the normal range (above 99 F or 37.2 C), the person should stay home or go home immediately and be monitored for other signs of sickness. It should be communicated with families that when children are sick at home, they are not to come to schools, and parents should report the sickness to schools right away. If a person is confirmed to have COVID-19, each classroom that the person has been a part of needs to close for 2 weeks before returning to face-to-face sessions.

2). Masks, Gloves, and Hand Washing

Each student, teacher, and school staff member must wear a mask in schools. Schools should have a good supply of disposable masks at hand so they can be provided to members of the school community when necessary. As with other aspects of new schools, each new expectation must be communicated to students with care. Some students will find mask wearing to be restraining and uncomfortable, and we want to be sympathetic about their feelings and experiences. But we should also be firm and explain the importance of this new practice, and how it will help everyone stay healthy. We must also show all students, in ways that they can understand, how they should not touch their faces, as viruses can enter their bodies easily through this contact. Though masks limit the conveyance of our facial expressions, we can learn to use sign language to communicate our feelings with each other (e.g., showing support, love, acknowledgement, agreement, and disagreement). Each school and classroom may work to invent their own system of gestures.

At this point during the pandemic, I would not recommend requiring small children not to touch each other on the playground and in other spaces, but regular hand washing should be required when they arrive to school in the morning and when they return from recess. Schools need to equip bathrooms with soap and paper towels and classrooms with hand sanitizer. Teachers must show students how to wash their hands thoroughly (for at least 20 seconds) and provide enough time for all students to wash their hands properly before coming into classrooms. This means that, depending on how many students are in a classroom and how many washing stations are available, it can take up to 5 minutes or more for students to wash their hands. Each teacher may want to create a set of transition activities to conduct while waiting for all students to complete hand washing.

3). Physical Distancing in Classrooms

We have seen many examples of how schools in different countries have attempted to safely distance students from each other (e.g., Denmark, the Netherlands). When there are 30 or more students in a small classroom, that can easily encourage viruses to move from one student to the next. Separating desks by 6 feet (2 meters) will be essential, and that means we will have to find extra space for all students in the school. One principal I interviewed shared how he is planning to expand classrooms into extra spaces within his school building, such as the gymnasium and outdoor spaces, and have non-classroom teachers (e.g., after-school program staff) teach lessons with small groups, while the main teachers remain responsible for planning and organizing learning activities. The instructional materials that were previously shared among students (e.g., pencils, counters) will instead be organized in separate packages for individual use.

Some schools may designate certain students to come to schools on certain days of the week, or certain parts of the day. For example, in Australia, when they started bringing students together in April, they used a staggered schedule of different groups of students attending one day per week. They believed that social and emotional connections to be important, and one day a week kept the essential relationships, while they tried to figure out the next steps.

Wisconsin Department of Education published a thorough guidelines for school reopening, including several possible physical models for their districts to consider. For example, one model suggests that half of students come Mondays and Thursdays, another group come Tuesdays and Fridays, while all students will engage in remote learning on days that they don't come to campus. This way, a number of students who will be in a physical classroom at one time can be managed, and each student will continue to learn. The district can then use Wednesdays for teacher professional development day as they anticipate teachers will require extra time to plan and coordinate hybrid teaching.

Aki Murata, Ph.D.

Some districts are requiring certain essential grade levels to physically return to school earlier than others. For example, one district has first and fifth graders in elementary school buildings return first, as they consider these are essential grades—first graders are learning how to participate in the school, and fifth graders are finishing elementary school. In these schools, students are spread out in multiple classrooms to maintain social distancing, and the schools plan to experiment with different aspects of the new setting before inviting back students in other grades, who will remain learning remotely for the first few months of the school year. In Denmark, as they reopened schools, the primary focus was on bringing back elementary grades first, then expanded it into secondary schools, taking advantage of empty classrooms and buildings in the process.

Lunch time becomes critical as students will take their masks off; it is safer for students to have lunch in their classrooms at their desks, or outside. Schools will want to instruct students on how to sanitize their own desks before lunch time (e.g., using disinfectant wipes) and provide special individual containers in which to keep masks while eating. Students should be reminded not to touch their masks while eating, as they can spread viruses that way.

4). Deep Cleaning of School Facilities

Each school shall establish new deep cleaning routines in the building to keep the facilities, furniture, and material sanitized every day.

Dimension 2: Academic Content

Except for the communities whose schools utilized cutting-edge technologies and private tutors for the last few months, most schools in the United States focused their remote teaching on reviewing the materials students had learned prior to the quarantine. That means the academic content that was supposed to be taught between March and June 2020 has not been touched in many schools. As an educational researcher and content expert, I believe it was a sound decision not to push academic learning in a time of confusion and trauma. I fully support how schools prioritized maintaining social and emotional connections over students' academic interests.

Now that we are faced with schools reopening, many teachers are feeling stressed anticipating how they will have to teach the content from the previous grades. As one elementary-school principal in Toronto, Richard, shared with me, as educators, we take a developmental approach by always starting where the students are in terms of their skill and knowledge development. And that can mean addressing the delay in terms of content learning. Schools are addressing this issue in different ways.

Some schools are having the previous grades' teachers continue to teach the same group of students. This has two benefits: 1) The teachers are familiar with the content and will start where students are, and 2) this will continue the classroom culture connection from the previous year, ensuring emotional safety. I believe this is a fantastic idea, one that shows how we value students and community. Content specialists at the district or national levels will work to come up with teaching plans for the academic year 2020–21 (and 21–22) to help bridge the content gap created during the quarantine.

For the teachers who are receiving students from lower level schools, such as Grade 6 middle-school teachers who are receiving Grade 5 students who are coming from elementary school, or Grade 9 high school teachers who are receiving Grade 8 students from middle school, the transitions may require more coordination and planning. One approach is to keep the students in the lower level schools with existing teachers for the first few months to get caught up with the previous year's content before starting the new academic year.

Some countries are discussing shifting the start of the academic year by a few months. For example, in the United States where our academic year typically starts in September, we may shift it to January, so students would have 4 months in the previous grade before moving on to their new grade.

Whatever we decide to do with academic content teaching, I want to emphasize that students will learn and get caught up with time. This message should be communicated up front with teachers, so they will not be overly stressed regarding their teaching, while they are also adjusting to new school expectations and settings. I believe academic content learning should be the last concern when it comes to schools reopening. As always, when students' needs are met, they will learn more as a result. According to our old normal, we are a few months behind right now, and we must accept that. When reopening schools, learning may be slow as everyone adjusts to the new expectations, but once students feel safe and secure, they will be motivated to learn, because learning is, after all, an innate human activity.

The "mile wide and inch deep" approach to education (in the United States) means we tend to skim the surface of many topics and teach without depth. Perhaps COVID-19 will teach us that we should cut down on the number of content topics and focus on doing a really good job with less content. One high school math teacher, Stephanie, mentioned that identification of "power standards" would be helpful for her and her colleagues, so they can focus on just a few core standards. I have no doubt that our reopened schools will better serve our students, but we should focus on quality over quantity: Hurrying the process will certainly not invite the best outcomes in the long run.

With the possibility of remote teaching continuing or hybrid teaching upon school reopening, teachers may consider taking advantage of a project-based curriculum. What it means is students are presented with a project topic (e.g., careers, animal lives, event planning, urban architecture), and given structured freedom to conduct own research and create a final product. Teachers must plan collaboratively and think of many directions students can take the project to, but it will ultimately allow freedom for students (and teachers) to work on their own pace for the days they don't come to schools. For example, students may research their ideal career; what they do, the training it requires, what they need to know, etc. They can write a research report (language arts), create a spreadsheet gathering the data on where people with the career are (geography), what academic degrees they have, etc. (math), and investigate the nature of the work, whether related to science or arts.

Dimension 3: Social and Emotional Care

As many of the educators I interviewed agreed, the social and emotional care dimension of the schools will be critical in reopening. Many students (and teachers) were surprised to be told to stay home in March as an extended spring break, and since then, they have received ever-changing expectations of "how to do school." They have been confused and uncertain. We hope that by this fall, our society will be at least semi-opened, and that our students can go outside of their homes for shopping, hiking, picnicking, and meeting with a few friends—with proper precautions. Students, along with educators, have received various messages and sometimes conflicting information about COVID-19 at home, and everyone will have many questions as they come back to school.

I will keep this section short, as I will be discussing this dimension in depth in latter chapters. I want to emphasize here how teachers must have a coordinated front for the returning students, holding space for them and communicating new expectations (and why such expectations are necessary) for a new school community. As many school administrators are aware, we must support teachers first, to make sure their emotional and social needs are met, so that they can (again) be the agents for the change. As a Grade 5 teacher in San Jose, Kristianna, said during her interview, she had played the role of the protector for her students in the past, when the current president was elected and then when there were school shootings in the news, and she felt confident she could do it again.

I also trust in our teachers, who have done tremendous work for the past few months, constantly changing their teaching approaches to keep up with evolving challenges while keeping their students' well-being a priority, even when they were also scared and uncertain.

Aki Murata, Ph.D.

CHAPTER 13. What We Missed During Remote Teaching

During interviews, both experienced and not-so-experienced teachers expressed their feelings that remote teaching is not real teaching. It reminded me of when I first started teaching online courses at the university level, how I felt it had nothing to do with what I thought teaching was, either. I am an educator who researches teaching and learning processes. I have taken pride in helping teachers of different career levels teach meaningfully by understanding how students learn. Online teaching had very little to do with what I had been teaching teachers. It took me a few years to see how good online courses are very different from face-to-face courses and how learning can be facilitated virtually as a very different kind of learning from what we do in person. In this chapter, I discuss good teaching in our old normal that we came to appreciate more during remote teaching.

The Beauty of Good Teaching (in Physical Classrooms)

Teachers help students create meaning in their learning. Though facts and procedures can be taught remotely, when the learning lacks social meaning, they can disappear from students' memories quickly. Carol, an early-elementary-grade teacher, mentioned in the interview how she was certain her students were learning new words, improving their adding skills, and tackling assigned activities (thanks to parents' help at home), but the sum of the collaborative learning is not anywhere close. Individually, students may be learning just as much, but when put together as a classroom community, the shared knowledge is much less than before.

Anyone who has spent time in classrooms recognizes the unspoken learning that happens between students. Students notice how their peers are doing, try to apply a peer's idea in their own work, and reevaluate and revise as they go. Teachers notice this learning and facilitate the process by bringing out student ideas, highlighting the "thinking in progress," and having the group think deeply together about the problem at hand. When a group of students thinks together, they are likely to bring their lived experiences with them — different learning from the past and ideas and experiences from outside of the classroom, which broadens and deepens all student learning.

During forced remote teaching and learning, many teachers lamented the lack of being able to witness student thinking in progress. Many remote teaching tools exist that allow students to submit and share their ideas in creative ways (e.g., recording their verbal explanations and posting them along with a solution drawing), but what we get to see tends to be the finished product, without the evidence of a back-and-forth thinking process, with various pauses before coming to the final answers. The true beauty of learning is in the process, and the teachers who were accustomed to capitalizing on that beauty for further and deeper learning felt ineffective when teaching remotely.

One elementary-school principal, Richard, described how good teachers are, in a way, like improv actors who do not follow provided scripts, but rather respond to the interest, strengths and needs of their students without judgement. Of course, there are effective teachers who follow scripts, or who were told to follow scripts by school administrators, but he was talking about these great teachers I was fortunate to have met in my life and continue to learn from. When a teacher has experienced or mastered the improvisational nature of teaching, skillfully, constantly, and spontaneously responding to student learning, it is exhilarating. It creates a space of vulnerability (which means it may be scary for novice teachers), and once a teacher experiences it and gains familiarity with it, they strive to create such opportunities in everyday teaching. The element of surprise is critical—it keeps them on their toes, creating greater joy when they indeed make connections with students over something that was unexpected to both of them. Remote teaching stripped these spontaneous moments away from teachers; many felt they had lost the art in their practice.

Classroom Culture

Many teachers I interviewed talked about the value of classroom culture. They explained how the culture they worked so hard to develop with the students in early parts of the academic year 2019-2020 helped them learn remotely. Some even said they could not imagine what they would have done if COVID-19 hit them in September (the beginning of the U.S. school year), without the grounding culture to bind them together.

Many teachers purposefully spend a great deal of time at the beginning of the school year to develop a trusting and safe classroom culture with students. The classroom is a special place for everyone in it, including the teacher, to feel valued and respected for who they are—how they think, how they feel, their interests and backgrounds, communities they come from, their religions and home cultures, and the colors of their skin and physical features. Once the trust starts to develop and when the teacher has confidence that no one will violate the respect and trust in the classroom community, students can then start to learn academic content in a genuine way.

Good teachers read the room as they enter it. They feel the emotion of every student and help regulate those emotions by providing the just right amount of support. The students who are in the room will soon learn how to do it with each other, too, and provide care and support, either physically, emotionally, or socially, without being asked. Once this practice is established in the classroom, it creates a comfortable setting where every person cares and is cared for. Students come back day after day and feel a sense of community, and that feeling is empowering.

Classrooms that had established a sense of community had an easier time (not easy, but easier) transitioning to remote teaching because the students "wanted to" continue to feel the sense of belonging in their lives. When teachers understand this and use it wisely, the desire to be together cultivates the desire to learn as learning activities are the primary form of being together in classrooms, and this desire to learn is the ultimate foundation of good teaching. When students care about their togetherness, about their peers and their teacher, they put effort into their learning when things are not perfect. Many teachers I interviewed described this, with different words and descriptions, and were appreciative of the classroom culture that motivated students to keep showing up.

Safe classrooms serve as an anchor in student lives, and when those physical anchors were taken away overnight with COVID-19, many teachers, students, and their families continued to work together because they valued the connections with each other. One third-grade teacher in Oakland, California, Erin, described her classroom as "a safety bubble," and explained how it was popped unexpectedly as they transitioned into remote teaching. Her students were not willing to let go of their connections with one another just because they could not come to schools physically, however. They showed up remotely and tried hard to learn despite limited opportunities.

Some teachers also talked about the trust families had with them, which made remote teaching possible. One fifth-grade teacher in Louisiana, Kristie, said that she had shared her phone number with families at the beginning of the school year. As they shifted to remote teaching, students started sending her pictures of their work via text messages. A second-grade teacher in California, Cassy, said how she had gained the trust of parents over the years by teaching different siblings within the same families. The parents depended on her for their children's well-being, and their communications became more frequent and stronger as they progressed with remote teaching.

Teaching Redefined in a Remote Context

Personally, it was a treat to talk with teachers about their experiences, probing into what they truly missed from their classrooms. Many great teachers often brushed it off when I mentioned the "magic" I witnessed in their classrooms. The beautiful aspects of good teaching should not be lost as we move forward to reopen schools in a new way. As experienced educators, we shall maintain, or even amplify, great teaching. Our students and teachers deserve that to be a part of our new normal.

Aki Murata, Ph.D.

CHAPTER 14. What We Learned During Remote Teaching

For this chapter, I want to focus my discussion on what we did well in remote teaching, and what parts of it we may be able to continue when schools reopen. Though many educators felt they practically had to reinvent the wheel when they switched to remote teaching, a lot of creative ideas came from the unanticipated shift, making us stop and admire our ingenuity. As there are always new things we can learn from any experience, I want to highlight some new practices and resources we created that can continue to be of use to us, regardless of what the future of education looks like.

New "Free" Virtual Learning Opportunities

When we were forced into quarantine, many businesses shifted online as well, as it was the only choice, and started providing services free. There were many such examples.

Following are several notable ones that we can continue to integrate with future school experiences.

1). Virtual Field Trips and Museums

This was a truly ingenious idea. Many public museums, state parks, and historical architectural buildings offered free virtual tours for teachers and students. Without leaving their homes, students could enjoy seeing art exhibits, observing large sea creatures, experiencing vast historical monuments, and witnessing interesting science experiments. If planned and used purposefully, these virtual experiences could be a part of students' lives in remote areas or in schools with prohibitive budgets, or any time it is not possible to take a physical trip.

2). Virtual Commencement (and Other Events) With Well-Known Mentors

Many of us watched former President Barack Obama give a graduation speech online in May 2020 and felt inspired. When pressed to stay at home, we made the most of the experiences, and creating virtual connections with people whom we may not typically have access to was a bonus. In the future, we can continue to have virtual connections with our heroes and mentors in this manner.

3). Virtual Connections with People Who may not Live Nearby

One Grade 5 teacher shared a classroom activity in which her students wrote essays on what professions they wanted to have when they grew up. The teacher posted a request on social media to solicit letters from people in those professions. It was a great success! The students received letters from a NASA astronaut, a congresswoman from DC, an archeologist in a Brazilian forest, and a music composer in Italy. The teacher's creative idea invited connections that would not have been possible in a physical sense, and letter writers were willing to take a few minutes to communicate.

4). Virtual Learning Tools

Virtual learning tools, such as Google Classroom, Seesaw, virtual whiteboards, and various conference/meeting software programs (e.g., Zoom, Skype, GoToMeeting) played major roles in remote teaching. Remote teaching will almost certainly continue, in some capacity, after schools reopen, and these tools will continue to support teachers and students.

Course Management Sites: Google Classroom, Canvas, and Blackboard are useful programs where teachers can post course ideas, assignments, and so on, and students can find all their information in one place. These sites can also become a portal for students to submit their assignments, helping teachers organize and manage their teaching efficiently. I would recommend teachers continue to at least keep the classroom site as an information depository and for students' on-demand electronic communication.

Virtual Whiteboards: Virtual whiteboards come in many forms, and many teachers learned to record their teaching as they wrote on the virtual boards in order to archive lessons for students to access remotely and asynchronously. As discussed in the previous chapter, this form of teaching tends to reinforce one-way knowledge transmission, without students' ongoing input and questions, so teachers should supplement virtual whiteboards with a separate space where learning can be more interactive (e.g., comments, Q&A). With some whiteboard tools, students can share their work in synchronous lessons, though sharing is typically limited to one student at a time.

Recording One's Own Teaching: There are several tools teachers can use to record their own teaching to post on their course site. For the simplest recording, teachers can use Quick Time (for Apple users) to "screen record" while they talk through their PowerPoint slides or other materials. Zoom has a recording function with which you can toggle between your own image and the screen share (e.g., PowerPoint slides, virtual materials, videos). One AP History teacher in Chicago, Andrea, shared how she had created a lesson (using Loom) where she talked through each student's answer to an AP exam question, explaining how they were graded, so the students could understand the expectations. This is a good example of creative remote teaching. Students can access a lesson asynchronously to watch, pause, think, rewind, and rewatch in ways that are helpful to them. If they can follow it up by asking personalized questions to the teacher, that will further enhance their learning.

Virtual Learning Portfolios: Seesaw and Flipgrid are popular teaching tools, and they have great potential for being used in new schools. Students can upload their work in formats that they choose (e.g., voice recording, video, drawings), allowing them to express ideas in creative ways. Again, the thinking-in-process tends to get lost in this approach, but teachers may use these portfolios to store student work for later use. Students can also respond to their peers' work by adding comments, and families can join the process by having separate access to the portfolios. One parent in California mentioned in the interview that she found her fourth-grade son viewing his friend's work and videos on Fripgrid multiple times during remote learning, because he missed the connections and friendship. While not a perfect solution, the virtual learning tools could help students and families maintain connection with each other.

Online Meeting Tools: Zoom and Google Meet are useful for classroom meetings, announcements, and short lessons. Many teachers who initially used these to simply lecture all day after shifting to remote teaching quickly learned that it would not be sustainable. Remote teaching is different from face-to-face teaching: face-to-face teaching requires a certain kind of creativity and interactions, and remote teaching requires partially using that creativity to foster different kinds of interactions. Simple top-down lectures, in either mode, will not work well.

In summary, virtual learning tools can be useful and can help support student learning if they are used creatively and mindfully, supplementing face-to-face teaching in reopened schools.

Individualized Remote Care and Connections for Mental and Emotional Health

Many schools and teachers created new ways to connect with students in remote teaching. Meeting with large groups of students all day long was no longer the norm, and teachers started reaching out to individual students for personal check-ins and counseling. One Grade 6 teacher said she makes sure she talks with each student once a week, even if that just means a few minutes of sharing how things are going at home. Each student needs to feel seen and heard by adults at schools, and this individualized connection can continue to be utilized in reopened schools. Especially when students' mental health is concerned, a time when each student can receive undivided attention from a teacher (or other school personnel) can be invaluable.

Some schools offered virtual meditation time and group therapy sessions. One parent even mentioned how her children's school offered a remote session with a therapy dog. When schools reopen, meditation and group therapy sessions can be integral parts of the new school day; these meetings can be scheduled in advance or offered as a drop-in during specific hours.

Flexible Schedules, Autonomy, and Independence

In the past, we tended to believe schools needed to function with rigid schedules and checklists. Remote teaching taught us that such expectations can be relaxed, and we still learned. In reopening schools, some students and parents may ask why they need to adhere to rigid schedules again after months of not having them. One high school teacher in Massachusetts, Stephanie, mentioned how she had learned that many of her students studied late at night, and that it wasn't unusual to have assignments come in at 2 am.

If we purposefully incorporate hybrid teaching by taking advantage of the positives of remote learning, we should be able to maintain built-in autonomy and independence within schools and allow more flexibility for student learning. If teachers post lesson materials on their classroom sites, students will be able to continue managing their  own learning by working when they want to between face-to-face learning sessions. It will free up teachers from having to be responsible for all aspects of student learning, and I see this as a positive change. In order to do this well, I see the value of collaboration among teachers. Instead of every teacher planning separate remote lessons; a grade-level group or subject-area team can post one lesson for the larger group of students. This will support teachers to learn about content more deeply and about student learning, by sharing questions and investigating solutions together. I see a great potential with this approach for the future.

CHAPTER 15. Stepping Up for Social and Emotional Health

As discussed in the previous chapters, all educators need to be on board to creatively reimagine our schools after COVID-19. Though I am seeing articles explaining the physical organization of schools, few have touched on the social and emotional health of students and teachers. In this chapter, I want to focus my discussion on it, as I believe this can become the key to the successful transition to new schools.

Where Students and Teachers Are Now

As I write this book (June 2020), many schools are ending their academic year remotely in the United States. There is definitely a sense of relief that remote teaching and learning is ending, and students can now switch gears to summer vacation mode, though "vacation" has a different meaning to many of us right now. In the past, students looked forward to being at home with families with somewhat more-relaxed schedules, visiting distant relatives, playing with friends for extended hours, or attending summer camps. This summer, many continue to stay home, and their daily activities may not change a whole lot.

Many teachers also feel relieved now, anticipating some down time and breaks from remote teaching, juggling work, home, and parenting responsibilities, while they also feel weary anticipating the upcoming changes when schools reopen. They may be reading emails from their school districts outlining the new physical guidelines for the fall. Many know the beginning of the school year is a critical time to develop safe classroom communities and wonder how all these new guidelines may (or may not) work with their normal community practices.

There is no question that all teachers and students will have some level of uncertainty when schools reopen. As principals or school administrators, it will be important to have guidelines in place so that teachers will know where to start when they return. And for that, we must start planning a summer professional development (PD) sessions soon, to prepare them for reopening. Many of our teachers are resilient, and they have played a role of the stable adult multiple times when things were uncertain in their students' lives before. I have no doubt that they will continue to do that with the new set of uncertainties. However, they also need support to do the job well.

School Counselors, Psychologists, and Mental Health Professionals

In reopening schools, it's imperative that school counselors, psychologists, and mental health professionals are central to our planning and to schools' daily operation. I cannot emphasize enough that social and emotional health needs to be addressed centrally, or every other effort we make in reopening schools will likely fall apart. When students feel afraid, they will not learn. When teachers feel endangered, they will not teach effectively.

In preparation for this book, I interviewed several school psychologists and counselors. They shared how they were reaching out to school communities, offering resources and support for teachers and parents. One school psychologist in Oakland, California, Alejandra, was holding webinars for school staff, focusing on topics of mental health and trauma and on how support should be provided when students show signs of posttraumatic stress at home and in remote teaching. This training will continue during summer PD and in reopened schools. In taking advantage of remote technology, schools may provide access to the archive of mental health resources for teachers and parents, so they will be able to learn how best to support students through new transitions.

During summer PD sessions, participants should brainstorm what questions students may bring to school reopening and become prepared to answer these questions; some questions are easier to answer than the others. For example, a second grader may ask if it is safe to play with their friends on the playground. We can answer, "YES, it is safe to play with friends, but you'll need to wear masks and wash your hands upon returning to classroom." A harder question might be, for example, a high school student feeling anxious whether it's safe to remain in a small-group when she knows another member of the group has gone to a party over the weekend. In answering this tough question, we may remind students to wear a mask and keep a safe distance apart from one another in the meeting, and when possible, finish the work remotely using online tools.

Because each family has subscribed to a different level of social distancing for months, it will feel strange for all of us to meet someone who has been more or less social than we have been during the pandemic so far. For example, some families have been strictly isolating and away from others for months (e.g., not stepping outside of the house, all groceries delivered), while other families might have been attending social events and getting together with close friends. Schools will have to determine what level of social distancing they will enforce, while realizing that students' family behaviors outside of the school are inconsistent and beyond the schools' control.

Upon reopening, school psychologists, counselors, and mental health professionals may offer extended accessibility for teachers and students, offering one-on-one counseling times when possible. Schools may create spaces for group counseling for students (and separately for teachers), where students and teachers can share their concerns, be assured that their feelings are normal, learn what is expected at schools, and be provided with tools and practices they can use. The process of seeking help (e.g., physical, emotional) should be explained and illustrated for students so that they will know how their concerns will be taken care of once expressed. Teachers must be informed how to guide different concerns coming from students to appropriate school staff (e.g., school nurse, psychologist) for different reasons. School psychologists, counselors, and mental health professionals who work at schools will also need extra support in doing their job well, as they will be taking on extra work and stepping into unknown territories.

In reimagining new school schedules, we may have outdoor meditation (or yoga) time, where teachers and students can spend a part of the day centering on calmness while maintaining a safe distance from one another.

Important Messages for Students

One parent in California, Judith, mentioned that she did not want her son's teacher to start the school year by instilling additional fear when he is already feeling anxious. The communication of new health practice expectations must be grounded in positivity, purposefulness, and safety. When students (and teachers) come to schools feeling uncertain, it's important to communicate the following messages upfront.

<u>You are safe</u>: In schools, our first priority is your safety. We are doing everything we can to keep you safe at school. When we determine safety cannot be promised, we will return to remote teaching and learning. All our new rules and expectations are to keep everyone safe, and with everyone helping one another and following the rules, we will be able to remain safe together.

We will take care of you no matter what: Though we are learning as we go, you can rely on us to take care of you physically, emotionally, and socially. If you are not feeling well, there are people ready and available to care for you at school. No matter what the concern is, it will be taken seriously. If you need help, there are easy ways to seek it.

We will find answers together: When questions arise, sometimes, adults may not have all the answers, but we will investigate and find answers together. We will teach ourselves to feel okay about not having immediate answers, and we will trust that we are learning together to find the best solutions possible for the school community.

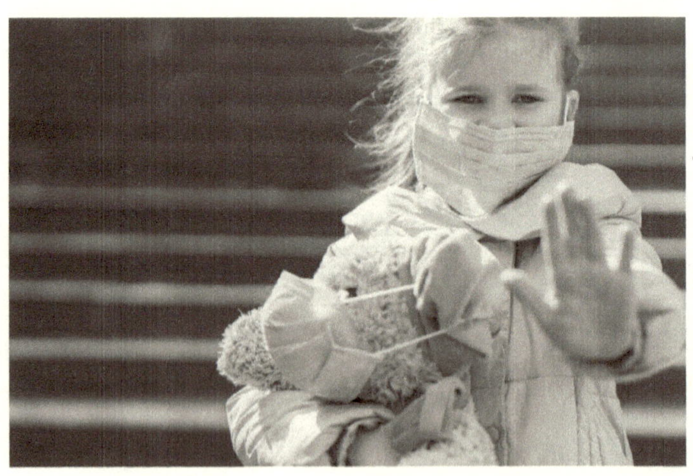

Aki Murata, Ph.D.

CHAPTER 16. Global Citizenship Education and Anti-Racism Education

When discussing diversity and multiculturalism, some schools celebrate differences without making connections to who they are. Several educators I interviewed expressed frustration in this regard. One educator in California, Mark, said equity is typically discussed in a tightly constrained manner at too many schools: it's talked about as an important topic, but there are no connections made to the privilege supporting these primarily white school communities. In many schools, colleges, and universities, they have diversity and inclusion committees and departments, and some do fantastic jobs recruiting and bringing students of diverse backgrounds (and feel successful doing it). But simply placing them in the existing racialized education settings would not readily make a difference – while gazing at the students if they would sink or swim. If we are serious about bringing different voices into our learning settings, we must change the ways we educate all of our students. Education is a part of the larger societal system, and when societal values are firmly on individual achievement and merit, empathy toward others can go counter to the core values. I want to suggest bringing diversity to the center of the discussion of school reopenings, as it showed up in many aspects of our lives during the pandemic.

Many school leaders are looking for meaningful ways to welcome back their students and teachers as they reopen schools. We all realize things won't be the same, and it is important to find a common ground on which to build our new school communities. Students and teachers are likely to have many uncertainties, and a reasonable place to start would be to make sure there are no unanswered questions from the pandemic remote teaching and learning period. In this chapter, I introduce the idea of global citizenship education and how it can help with reopening transitions.

Global citizenship education starts with how each student has a place on the earth, being connected to each other. Who they are matters, and their actions make differences for others even when they have never met each other.

> *It empowers each student with the agency to influence.*

The Reasons for the Remote Learning

Students will need to understand "why" they were learning remotely for the past several months. They have, of course, heard about COVID-19 and the quarantine, but as they come back to campus, schools will have an opportunity, as a community, to ground the reasons. The last thing we want is to leave our students wondering why and remain fearful of it happening again. Helplessness is our enemy, because it strips away student motivation and focus.

While students were staying home and learning remotely, they were indeed helping the world by not spreading the virus. Each day they stayed in mattered, and it helped someone else, whether living in the same neighborhood or another part of the world, stay healthy. Depending on the age of students, teachers may bring out the "flattening the curve" graphs we became so familiar with during the quarantine, which show how social distancing helped control the pandemic by reducing the number of COVID-19 cases, allowing hospitals to better handle their existing patients. Another way to show students how their quarantine made a difference in the world would be to compare graphs of different countries and states, revealing how social distancing helped different communities (and why).

Each time they washed their hands, each time they wore masks outside, each time they talked with friends via video chat instead of in person, these small acts contributed to managing the virus all over the world. This message is very important as we welcome students back to school. It celebrates how far they have come and shows them how we will continue to contribute to the wellness of all people of the world.

Schools may coordinate communications with other schools in different states or countries to share how their experiences with remote teaching and learning might have been similar and different, using virtual meeting functions we have all become very familiar with so far. With this kind of correspondence, acknowledge and celebrate what each student did, no matter how small, and how it influenced the wellness of the global community. Viruses are invisible and transmit silently and rapidly. That creates a sense of helplessness because we don't know when or how it might affect us. But we can flip this invisibility into a strength: Even though we can't see the virus, our everyday actions make a difference. Even though we may not see the effort, we can still fight it.

Older students may be encouraged to conduct their own research on different aspects of national and state policy that reduced the number of COVID-19 cases in their areas. Younger students may write letters to distant friends or relatives, explaining what they have been doing that's helping manage the spread of the virus and keep everyone healthy.

Strengthening Connections in School Communities

Global citizenship does not only mean connections to unknown others on the other side of the earth. The connections start in neighborhood and classroom communities. If we can make a difference in the world, we can definitely make one in our own communities. We cannot take it lightly that many students would come back to school after hearing various family and community discussions about COVID-19 and race. One middle school math teacher, Je Un, shared with me how one of her White students asked if the reason why White people are less likely to die because of the virus was "survival of the fittest," That became an invitation for her, the student, and his parents, to discuss more thoroughly about the virus, social systems, and inequity. As discussed in previous chapters, communities of color were hit harder by the virus because of the existing inequitable social system in the United States, and no student is too young to start having conversations on racism (many age-appropriate resources are available).

Though school is a reflection of society, and students bring to the classroom what they hear off campus, as always, educators have a power to influence students' understanding of the world. Each student can make a difference for others, and they can certainly make a bigger difference for friends and peers.

Anti-Racism Education

Global citizenship education must go hand-in-hand with anti-racism education, and this is how I suggest schools start the work. As a part of professional development meetings, teachers and school staff can collaboratively examine their beliefs and practices surrounding race. Using a scenario or case, teachers can explore how certain beliefs and practices they have may be grounded in racism and racist mindset.

Aki Murata, Ph.D.

Have a focused discussion on systemic racism in the United States, and how and why White people benefit just by being White, because the system takes advantage of people of color. Set a ground rule and expectations that everyone is learning about how to appropriately discuss racism, and no shaming in the discussions. Educators need to learn to identify race-based decision making for creating more-equitable schools. Identify microaggressions in everyday interactions, bring the examples for open discussion, and emphasize how students of color experience these interactions.

What does valuing Black lives mean in the everyday lives of educators? It means that teachers need to consciously reflect on their practices. They need to ensure that the Black students are seen, and their voices are heard. To start out, teachers may want to video record a typical lesson, and later watch it and count how many times White students and students of color spoke up in the video. When only White students are speaking in discussions, we must change the way we teach to make room for different voices. If Black students are involved in activities, teachers should be extra conscious that they are not suppressed by others in the group and that their ideas are equally heard. As teachers, we have the moral responsibility to bring Black voices to classroom learning.

Teachers must consciously reflect on what differences they can make to facilitate the learning process for all students.

If educators together work on their own development as anti-racists while guiding global citizenship awareness among students, we will be able to create schools that celebrate and value student diversity in a truer sense.

Global Citizenship Education Practices and Activities

In each classroom, students can research and bring a current event/topic to discuss. They can discuss what they are doing (or can do) related to the current event to help make a positive difference. For younger students, teachers can utilize children's books that address appropriate topics, or bring relevant topics from current events, so students can make connections and feel empowered for being able to help in their own ways.

Any topics that cultivate and nurture connections between students and the outside world are important. It will be a great place to start by identifying student actions that make a difference.

Facilitating REAL Empathic Conversations in Classrooms

Aki Murata, Ph.D.

The core of global citizenship is <u>empathy</u> and <u>making authentic connections</u>. In classrooms, we can start building these connections by creating a time to share and listen to personal stories. Many teachers already do this every day, and I wanted to give some guidelines here for successful facilitation of empathic conversations.

In a diverse classroom, the diversity provides a great opportunity for students to share and hear different life stories and develop empathy. In a more homogeneous classroom, we can also create opportunities for sharing personal stories for empathy.

Teachers should provide basic expectations for the conversations and model how to actively listen to others' stories:

- We do not interrupt when someone is talking.
- Do not offer solutions unless asked.
- Listen and try to understand the person's experience in their own words (without making connections to your personal experiences too quickly)
- Try to imagine how it must feel to be in the person's position. (That's empathy!)

Example of facilitating a REAL empathic conversation:

1. The teacher brings up an authentic topic. If something is going on in a student's life, that makes the topic relevant. Or, the teacher may bring up a bigger social problem, such as police brutality.
2. One student is allowed to speak at a time, in their own voice, without interruption.
3. Before suggesting a solution or making a connection to a similar experience, another student repeat the speaker's experience in their own words and ask the original speaker if they expressed it accurately (if not, the conversation loops back).
4. Take a moment to feel the emotion as a group. Empathize. Do not move away from the speaker's experience right away. While some students may have different opinions or experiences, focus on the original speaker's experience. This is not the time to present a different perspective.
5. Share feelings. Have the original speaker acknowledge these feelings if possible, or this sharing can happen without making the speaker further vulnerable. Hand gestures may be helpful in expressing agreement and support.
6. The teacher asks the original speaker if there is anything else they want to add. If not, they can choose the next

speaker, who would start by sharing how they felt in hearing the original speaker's experience, and why they want to share their ideas or experience because there is a connection.

7. The process repeats (though one person speaking may be enough for one conversation).

For my dissertation research, I collected data in Japanese Grade 1 classrooms. Japanese culture, in general, is very relational and emotion-oriented, and I could witness how small children learned to have the empathic conversation as a group. In the classroom, students discussed about an important topic (for them) every morning, and the conversation sometimes lasted for hours. For example, they talked about the incident in the playground from the day before, or how they thought the practice for the school play was going. The teacher patiently led each student express feelings, while he sometimes gave me a side smile showing how he wanted to get on with the math lesson soon.

Teachers may try the empathic conversation during summer PD, always using authentic and real problems, and focus on feelings. They may be surprised how long the conversation can last on one topic, and if they really focus on feelings, how different opinions and disagreements won't matter in the end. Emotions connect people together — not differing experiences and ideas.

Black Lives Matter

We are currently in a critical time in the history, and we can use the momentum to educate our students to create a more just racial community for the future. Each school should come with their own strong statement regarding Black Lives Matter (see Chapter 10 for an in-depth discussion of this movement). This is not the space to entertain different opinions. We all value each other's lives, and Black lives need to be elevated right now because they are not treated equitably otherwise.

Regardless of student ages, White privilege should be explained in ways that they understand, and include how White students and teachers must do more to acknowledge Black students (and other students of color) in the classroom. Older students may have a focused discussion of how privilege works in our lives, and how White people can benefit by not doing anything. Thus, it is White people's responsibility to equalize the field by paying extra attention to Black voices and experiences. Students may design, plan, and facilitate community projects to help persons of color in the area (or elsewhere) by first learning their needs. This initial step is very important, as each community's needs are very different. Students can then research how best to help meet the needs, and create a project to help the community.

For younger students, there are many books available for children that celebrate differences among us. They are a great place to start. By discussing the stories in the book, teachers can guide students' attention to how they are also celebrating differences in the classroom and community. Racism usually happens when White people treat people of color badly, and it has to stop. In line with global citizenship, young students can take part by playing and working with their classmates who may look differently from them. Teachers can plan activities that celebrate differences (instead of ignoring them) and emphasize how we all learn more when different ideas are shared. When they notice bullying on the playground or elsewhere, based on race or otherwise, students should know it is important for them to talk to trusting adults (parents, teachers), so they can intervene.

Racism is learned, and we continue to learn about it and about ourselves every day. No one is perfect when it comes to race relations, and making a mistake does not make you a racist, but it simply means you have more to learn. People of color usually know more about racism, simply because they have experienced it more. White people need to try harder to learn about racism and change their thinking and behavior. Empathic conversations also help. It is important to create and maintain a space where mistakes are expected, and when they are pointed out, we simply thank the person who pointed them out and move forward, so we can all learn together.

Learning More About Global Citizenship Education and Anti-Racism Education

There will be another book about Global Citizenship Education and Anti-Racism Education that follows. Please get in touch with me if you (and your schools) are interested in learning more about it. I am happy to continue the conversation with you.

Aki Murata, Ph.D.

Conclusion

n imagining our schools 10 years from now, we can hear educators discussing what they learned during the COVID-19 pandemic and how that made their schools better. We are standing in the historical crossroads together, with the unusual opportunity to reinvent education. We owe it to our students and hard-working teachers to take advantage of this and steer ourselves toward better schools.

We develop deeper connections as humans when things are not easy. We empathize with each other's experiences and grow together. COVID-19 indeed shocked us with its arrival, but we have come this far making many changes already. In conducting comparative education research projects, I learned that while it is interesting to study different policy decisions and instructional practices in different cultures, certain orientations to ideas always highlighted the unique values and beliefs of a culture. Seeing how different countries are handling the school closings and reopenings, we learn what we truly value in our students' education (and what we don't). It is a good time to reflect, as educators, on what is important to us — do we avoid uncomfortable conversations, quickly forget what happened during the pandemic, and strive to gain back the old normal? Or do we take time to learn from our experiences, however uncomfortable they were, have brave conversations, and create a stronger educational community moving forward together? The latter approach will without doubt invite more mistakes and uncertainties, but we have come this far already, didn't we? And we've got each other. This is a great time to make important differences.

As this book is published in summer 2020, we have a few weeks before our next academic year starts. I look forward to seeing creative ideas abound in the process of reinventing schools, and I feel grateful to be sharing the experiences with other educators.

Let's rise up together…!

Suggested Additional Readings

Readings about School Reopening

California Department of Education. (2020). Stronger together: A guidebook for the state reopening of California's public schools. *California Department of Education.* Retrieved July 12, 2020 from https://www.cde.ca.gov/ls/he/hn/documents/strongertogether.pdf

Centers for Disease Control and Prevention. (2020). *Considerations for Schools.* Retrieved July 12, 2020 from https://www.cdc.gov/coronavirus/2019-ncov/community/schools-childcare/schools.html

Giannini, S., Jenkins, R., Saavedra, J. (2020). Reopening schools: When, where and how? *UNESCO.* Retrieved July 12, 2020 from https://en.unesco.org/news/reopening-schools-when-where-and-how

Melnick, H. Darling-Hammond, L., Leung, M., Yun, C., Schachner, A., Piasencia, S., & Ondrasek, N. (2020). Reopening schools in the context of COVID-19: Health and safety guidelines from other countries. *Learning Policy Institute.* Retrieved July 12, 2020 from https://learningpolicyinstitute.org/product/reopening-schools-covid-19-brief

Wisconsin Department of Public Instruction & Educational Stakeholders and the Wisconsin Department of Health Services. (2020). Education forward: Reopening Wisconsin schools. *WDPI.* Retrieved July 12, 2020 from https://dpi.wi.gov/sites/default/files/imce/sspw/pdf/Education_Forward_web.pdf

Readings about Remote Teaching

Busteed. B. (2020). Schools must both reopen and continue online. *Forbes.* Retrieved July 12, 2020 from https://www.forbes.com/sites/brandonbusteed/2020/05/05/schools-must-both-re-open-and-continue-online/#2c8930345d98

Cipriano, C. & Brackett, M. (2020). Teachers are anxious and overwhelmed. They need SEL ow more than ever. *EdsSurge.* Retrieved July 12, 2020 from https://www.edsurge.com/news/2020-04-07-teachers-are-anxious-and-overwhelmed-they-need-sel-now-more-than-ever

Goldstein, D. (2020). The class divide: Remote learning at two schools, public and private. *The New York Times.* Retrieved July 12, 2020 from https://www.nytimes.com/2020/05/09/us/coronavirus-public-private-school.html?searchResultPosition=5

Goldstein, D. (2020). Research Shows Students Falling Months Behind During Virus Disruptions. *The New York Times.* Retrieved July 12, 2020 from https://www.nytimes.com/2020/06/05/us/coronavirus-education-lost-learning.html

St. George, B., Natamson, H., Stein, P. & Lumpkin, L. (2020). Schools are shut, so how will kids learn amid the covid-19 pandemic? *The Washington Post.* Retrieved July 12, 2020 from https://www.washingtonpost.com/local/education/schools-are-shut-so-how-will-kids-learn-amid-the-covid-19-

pandemic/2020/03/22/dac4742e-6ab7-11ea-9923-
57073adce27c_story.html

The World Bank. (2020). How countries are using edtech
(including online learning, radio, television, texting) to support
access to remore learning during the COVID-19 pandemic. *The
World Bank*. Retrieved July 12, 2020 from
https://www.worldbank.org/en/topic/edutech/brief/how-countries-
are-using-edtech-to-support-remote-learning-during-the-covid-19-
pandemic

Wyman. C. (2020). Difficult home lives and the other side of
educational access. *Inside Higher Ed*. Retrieved July 12, 2020
from
https://www.insidehighered.com/advice/2020/05/14/teaching-
students-difficult-home-lives-during-pandemic-opinion

Readings about COVID-19 and Social Disparity

Boule. J. (2020). Why Coronavirus is killing African-Americans
more than others? *The New York Times*. Retrieved July 12, 2020
from
https://www.nytimes.com/2020/04/14/opinion/sunday/coronavirus
-racism-african-americans.html?searchResultPosition=8

Burch, A. D. S. (2020). Why the virus is a civil-rights issue: The
pain will not be shared equally. *The New York Times*. Retrieved
July 12, 2020 from
https://www.nytimes.com/2020/04/19/us/coronavirus-civil-
rights.html?searchResultPosition=1

Chotinerm I. (2020). The interwoven threads of inequality and
health. *The New Yorker*. Retrieved July 12, 2020 from

https://www.newyorker.com/news/q-and-a/the-coronavirus-and-the-interwoven-threads-of-inequality-and-health

Guterres. A. (2020). "The pandemic is exposing the exploiting inequalities of all kinds, including gender inequality: *United Nations.* Retrieved July 12, 2020 from https://www.un.org/en/un-coronavirus-communications-team/pandemic-exposing-and-exploiting-inequalities-all-kinds-including

Oppel Jr., R. A, Gebeloft, R., Lai, K.K.R., Writing, W., & Smith, M. (2020). The fuller look yet at the racial inequality of Coronavirus. *The New York Times.* Retrieved July 12, 2020 from https://www.nytimes.com/interactive/2020/07/05/us/coronavirus-latinos-african-americans-cdc-data.html

Pinsker, J. (2020). The pandemic will cleave American in two. *The Atlantic.* Retrieved July 12, 2020 from https://www.theatlantic.com/family/archive/2020/04/two-pandemics-us-coronavirus-inequality/609622/

Readings about Education Inequality

Anyon, J. (1980). Social class and the hidden curriculum of work. *Journal of education*, 67-92.

Anyon, J. (2014). *Radical possibilities: Public policy, urban education, and a new social movement.* Routledge.

Darling-Hammond, L. (2015). *The flat world and education: How America's commitment to equity will determine our future.* Teachers College Press.

Delpit, L. (2006). *Other people's children: Cultural conflict in the classroom.* The New Press.

Kozol, J. (2012). *Savage inequalities: Children in America's schools*. Broadway Books.

Lipman, P. (2004). *High stakes education: Inequality, globalization, and urban school reform.* Psychology Press.

Readings about White Privilege

DiAngelo, R. (2018). *White fragility: Why it's so hard for white people to talk about racism.* Beacon Press.

Kendi, I.X. (2017). *Stamped from the beginning: The definitive history of racist ideas in America.* Bold Type Books.

Oluo, Ijeoma. (2019). *So you want to talk about race*. Seal Press.

Aki Murata's Other Scholarly Work Related to This Book

Murata, A. (2016). Interactions between teaching and learning mathematics in elementary classrooms. In D. Scott & E. Hargreaves (Eds.). *Handbook of Learning*. London, England: SAGE. pp. 233-242.

Murata, A. (2013). Diversity and high academic expectations without tracking: Inclusively responsive instruction. *The Journal of Learning Sciences*, 21(2). 312-335. doi:10.1080/10508406.2012.682188

Murata, A. (2006). Bridging identities: Making sense of who we are becoming to be. In T. R. Berry and N. D. Mizzelle. (Eds.). *From oppression to grace: Women of color and their dilemma in academy*. NY: Stylus. pp. 24-33.

Murata, A., Siker, J., Kang, B., Kim, H-J., Baldinger, E. M., Scott, M., & Lanouette, K. (2017). Math talk and student strategy trajectories:

The case of two first grade classrooms. *Cognition and Instruction*. 35(4).
336-362. DOI:10.1080/07370008.2017.1362408.

Helgevold, N. & Murata, A. (2019). Problematizing teaching: Shifting preservice teacher talks through lesson study in Norway and the United States. In A. E. Lopez & E. L. Olan. (Eds). *Transformative pedagogies for teacher education: Moving towards critical praxis in an era of change*. Information Age. pp. 1-18.

Aki Murata, Ph.D.

Appendix: Interview Methods and Participant Information

Although this is not meant to be an academic book, I am a trained and experienced educational researcher. I believe it is important to provide the information on how the information was collected to write this book.

At the end of April 2020, I created social media posts (Facebook and Instagram), asking for educators and others who are concerned about education to virtually meet with me via Zoom for 30 min to share their remote teaching and learning experiences. I received more than 100 responses, and conducted 59 interviews altogether. Most interviewees were classroom teachers, but I also spoke to school principals, school district personnel, school personnel, and parents. I will provide the simple demographics of the interviewees below.

While we planned to speak for approximately 30 minutes, most interviews lasted longer (up to 45-60 min), and one extended to 120 minutes. One interview was conducted with two teachers together, and one principal was interviewed twice as I needed additional information from them. I did not record the interviews, but did take careful notes on conversations.

For each interview, I always started with an open-ended question, *"how have your experiences been with COVID remote teaching and learning?"* As the interviewee shared the experience, I then asked probing questions when unclear. At the end of every interview, I asked if it would be OK to include the experiences they shared with me in the book, and if so, I told them I would follow up with my write-up for their approval (and I subsequently did so). I also asked each interviewee later on via email if it would be ok to acknowledge them in the book, and if so, how they wanted to be acknowledged (e.g., name and location).

Genders of the Interviewees:
    Male: 5
    Female: 54
    <u>Total: 59</u>

How Interviewees Identified Themselves:
    Teachers: 35
    Principals: 4
    School Psychologists/Counselors: 3
    District Personnel" 1
    School Personnel: 3
    Teacher Educators: 6
    Parents: 3

Education-Related Businesses: 4
<u>Total: 59</u>

Teachers' School Levels:
    Elementary School: 31
    Middle School: 1
    High School: 3
    <u>Total: 35</u>

Acknowledgments

I would like to acknowledge all the educators and parents who are supporting their students' and children's learning during and beyond COVID-19 pandemic. I would especially like to acknowledge the following people (among others who preferred not to be publicly acknowledged) whose ideas are the foundation of this book:

Q Tien Le, San Francisco Unified School District; Stephanie Niedziela, Southwick MA; Monica Bhatachaya, STEP11, NYC; Zdenka Petrova; Dr. Rachel Orgel; Elizabeth K Baker, Mills College, Oakland, CA; Erin Ronhovde; Alejandra Ojeda-Beck, Berkeley, CA; Toby Wu, Brooklyn, NY; Judith Fabrega; Dr. Shelley Friedkin, Senior Research Associate, Mills College, Oakland, CA; Rebecca Fox, San Francisco; Andrea, Chicago; Yueh Mei, Singapore; Melissa Frost; Richard Messina, Principal, Dr. Eric Jackman Institute of Child Study Lab School, OISE, University of Toronto; Dr. Bindu E. Pothen; Toni Allen, NBCT, SF Bay Area; Jeremy Blinn – President, Florida Association of Science Supervisors; Coach Mark Kelley, Twin Lakes Academy Middle School, Jacksonville, Florida; Mark Basnage; Jody Siker; Laura; Kristie Hendricks; Cassandra Cuellar, Elkhorn Elementary, Castroville, CA; Charlotte, San Mateo; Darlynthia Smith, Educational Leader; Nikki, LCSW, School Social Worker; Lisa Dorner, University of Missouri; Hee-Jeong Kim, Hongik University, Korea; Je Un Park, math teacher, Philadelphia, PA; Dr. Maria Mendiburo, Microsoft:

Aki Murata, Ph.D.

Early Praises

Dr. Aki Murata has done educators and education leaders a great service in mapping out the outlines of what COVID has done to our schools and students, and how we might build more resilient and equitable schools in response. Starting with a look at the human side of all the COVID disruption in the early Spring of 2020, she pivots to an exploration of concrete ideas and big principles we should keep in mind as we gear up for an uncertain 2020-21 school year. If you've had the fortune of working with or studying with Dr. Murata, you know there are few people better suited to navigating the pedagogical, logistical, and human aspects of this crisis and our response.
-- Mark Basnage

An inspirational read on how this is the perfect time in our country to work together on addressing the inequities in our education system. Dr. Murata expertly weaves together the experiences of teachers as they shift to remote teaching. She highlights best practices from both the old normal of teaching in traditional classrooms and the new normal of schooling at home. With a hopeful message on how we can emerge from a challenging time with a better education for all of our students, this book is a must-read!
-- Dr. Bindu Pothen

In her book 'Reopening Better Schools', Aki Murata creates an easy-to-read and solutions-focused narrative for educators and parents. The writing flows seamlessly, acknowledging the complex landscape teachers had to navigate in the early days of COVID-19, describing their creative remote-teaching methods that met all

students' needs, to presenting practical recommendations for educators, administrators, and districts. Aki Murata's powerful prose urges her readers to recognize this time as a golden opportunity to reinvent education for the better. This is a must-read for parents as well, who worry that their children have fallen behind. This book will reassure them their children will learn the content, but what is much more important is ensuring students' optimal mental health, and the need for developing an anti-racist, relevant, and global curriculum, which will ultimately lead to empowered and informed citizens of the future.
-- Monica Bhattacharya, STEP11. NYC

What is so hopeful about this text is that Aki has managed to authentically portray the lives and work of teachers during the initial challenges of responding to CV-19 and also the lived context of BLM for teachers and their students. The emotions, fears, hard work, worries, successes, near-misses and hopes are told through "Mia" in the first part of the text. What follows next brings to the foreground the possibilities for change for all of us involved in schooling. This rich approach to telling the story of the Spring 2020 with empathy and the eye of a patient Educational Researcher is critical at this time. I will use this text in my teacher education courses this Fall!
-- Elizabeth K Baker, Mills College, Oakland, CA

Few scholars in the field of education reside so comfortably at the intersection of research and practice. As a practitioner and a researcher, Dr. Murata grounds the book in her deep knowledge of pedagogy, racial and social inequities, and teacher practice. Her recommendations are applicable to a variety of school settings, and I appreciate her foregrounding the movement for Black lives. A book about re-opening schools would not be complete without a thorough discussion about how schools,

intentionally or unintentionally, exacerbate racial/ethnic inequities and how we may envision a more racially just learning environment.
-- Q. Tien Le, San Francisco, San Francisco Unified School District

Amazing read! Reopening Better Schools, has captured a time in education that is an amalgamation of voices from stakeholders of various backgrounds. This collaboration has surfaced a plan of logic, safety, and social emotional sensibility that is also a tribute to hardworking, loving, educators across the United States. Dr. Murata has identified the need to emphasize "we must support our teachers first, to make sure their emotional and social needs are met, so they can (again) be the agents of change."
-- Jeremy Blinn, President, Florida Association of Science Supervisors

In this timely publication, Reopening Better Schools: Unexpected Ways COVID-19 Can Improve Education, Aki Murata reimagines how schools can be safely reopened in a way that addresses students' academic needs as well as their social and emotional ones. I especially appreciate how she honors educators' voices and experiences, which are often not considered when decisions are made about schools by state and local politicians; and that her analysis addresses the needs of Black, Indigenous, and other students of color who have been disproportionately affected by COVID-19. I highly recommend this book!
-- Melissa Frost

A marvelous book summarizing and detailing true accounts of how this pandemic has and is affecting the communities and schools. It is concisely written with great precision - an art not easy to master, for a situation that covers and affects so many facets of life. The school and life account of Mia sums up many experiences educators all around the world have faced and still facing. Even in

Singapore, I am sure Mia's story resonates with educators here. Thank you, Aki, for spending time listening to educators and parents, and documenting this historic unprecedented pandemic that we are going through, many lessons that we are still learning and will be lessons to be learnt going forward.
-- Yueh Mei, Singapore

Great overall assessment in this book. The changes in education due to Covid-19 has been a stark reminder of the importance of social services and support for students, including guidance and mentorship from educators. Students need structure.
-- Coach Mark Kelley. Twin Lakes Academy Middle School. Jacksonville, Florida

Dr. Murata is a true educator. Her understanding, respect, and admiration for other professionals in the field are unbound. As the stories of teachers, principals, school psychologists, and parents are shared at six-weeks into the pandemic, we gain insight into the changes needed to reopen better schools. This book elicits an urgent call to action and provides a coherence framework to rebuild stronger school communities.
-- Dr. Shelley Friedkin, Senior Research Associate, Mills College, Oakland, CA

Dr. Aki Murata bundles her expertise with many educators' experiences to show a cohesive narrative of our closures last spring before creating a focused front to meet emotional, physical, and educational challenges within a Covid-threatened classroom. She encourages readers to serve students first. The book is both encouraging and helpful in navigating our newest normal in schools.
-- Kristie M. Hendricks

As a teacher and a parent, I have many concerns around physical safety, social and emotional well-being, academic learning, and racial inequities as we re-open schools this fall in the midst of a global pandemic. But as Dr. Murata points out, despite our great challenges--or perhaps because of them--we also have an opportunity for positive change. Reopening Better Schools weaves together many of the threads that educators are facing in classrooms across the country at this unique cross-roads and encourages us to come together to reflect on our experiences, challenge our assumptions, and hopefully create stronger educational communities that better serve all of our students moving forward.
-- Caitlin Kline, Elementary School Teacher in Colorado

This book is necessary for teachers who are essential to our society in this pandemic era. As we can't imagine whether or not our students can go back to normal schools, we can think, through this book, our reopening schools with many different eyes such as teachers, students, parents, and principals As the schools in my society have reopened, I notice that this book also informs how American schools--where there are more complex social issues have-- can reopen .
-- Hee-Jeong Kim, Hongik University, Korea

Everybody should read this book, not only educators. I appreciated that it focuses on the positives, explaining that this situation has (hopefully) helped us to question the current education system and has brought a new opportunity for "re-opening" better schools that meet all students' needs.
-- Judith Fabrega

Thank You!

I appreciate your interests, curiosities, and/or contributions to the ideas expressed in this book. Books could not be meaningful without people reading them, thinking further about them, and talking about them, and you are the true engine to keep spreading the ideas into the future. Thank you.

If you are curious about the ideas shared in this book and wish to have a conversation with me, as a reader of the book, you'll get **a FREE 30-minute consultation,** virtually (via zoom) or on the phone. We may talk about your school's current situation, reopening plans, PD ideas (before, during, and after school reopening), etc. I am an experienced PD designer and provider (please read my bio in this book), and am happy to work with you in any capacity. I am a dynamic and empathic speaker and facilitator of learning, and enjoy working with educators. Please email me directly, *aki@akimurata.com,* and visit my web site for more information for this. *www.akimurata.com*.

More than anything, I THANK YOU for the continuing hard work as educators and parents. My sincere appreciations for the differences you make every day.

Aki Murata, Ph.D.
aki@akimurata.com
www.akimurata.com

About the Author

Aki Murata, Ph.D. is an educator, writer, and speaker who is best known for her research on mathematics teaching and learning and teacher development through lesson study. After obtaining Ph.D. from Northwestern University in 2002, she received a prestigious AERA-IES post-doctoral fellowship for three years, then held a professorship at Stanford University and UC-Berkeley. She has been sought to give plenary keynote speeches at many professional conferences and meetings as an education expert, and published many books and articles in top-level peer-reviewed journals. She has also received a Best Teaching Award and a Best Advising Award while at Stanford University, as recognitions for her personal approaches to mentor next generation of educators.

She managed multiple research projects on how mathematics teaching and learning interact and improve in elementary-school classrooms, and the results are now widely found in different textbooks and curriculum materials . She is passionate about helping teachers improve instruction, and facilitates lesson study (collaboration-based teacher professional development) globally, collaborating with educators at different career levels (e.g., preservice, inservice, instructional coaches) and in different subject areas. Originally from Japan, Aki brings a comparative lens to examine how teachers improve teaching by understanding their students' learning. Being an immigrant female scholar of color, she is committed to improve school experiences of students of color and strive to help educators at different levels and in various contexts.

Aki Murata, Ph.D.

Global Citizenship Education Press